MAN TO GOD

TRUTH OR FICTION

FASSAN RAMSARAN

 FriesenPress

Suite 300 - 990 Fort St
Victoria, BC, V8V 3K2
Canada

www.friesenpress.com

ISBN
978-1-5255-6868-8 (Hardcover)
978-1-5255-6869-5 (Paperback)
978-1-5255-6870-1 (eBook)

1. BODY, MIND & SPIRIT, MYSTICISM

Distributed to the trade by The Ingram Book Company

Table of Contents

Dedication

This volume is dedicated to my beloved guru, Paramahansa Yogananda, whose theoretical and practical teachings are the bedrock, without which none of this would have been possible. And also to the avatar, Sri Sathya Sai Baba, in whose holy presence I was blessed to spend several days of this mortal life. (Both of whom I am sure, in some mystical way, were instrumental in allowing me to complete this work.)

Preface

There have been many books written about the topics covered in this volume—and they have been around for a long time. Yet, they are not the flavors of the month. There seems to be a lack of connection between them and a failure to clarify what they truly represent.

The author is hereby trying to remove the mystery, make the reading easier, and unveil the hidden meanings behind these things being written about.

As how I came to write this book, that in itself, is hard to explain. Never in a lifetime or in a million years did I think of doing what I am doing now. Maybe that's stretching it a little too far, for stranger things have happened. There is no doubt a hidden hand is at play, (call it what you will), in the unfoldment of this work. I think a little background should give credence to this.

It was just after midnight, on September 15, 2012; I had just finished my nightly meditation, and I had flipped on the radio to my favourite programme, to kill some time before I went to sleep. I usually did this, as the material on the show dealt with the paranormal, the unexplained, and conspiracy theories, and I found it quite entertaining. (As a matter of fact, this is a top-rated show with a world-wide audience.) Anyway, there was a lively discussion taking place between the host and the guest. And they were talking about the hereafter. Although, the host had always seemed so quite knowledgeable on these subjects, after listening for about five minutes, it dawned on me that he wasn't really sure what he believed in.

And I realized if this was so hard for him, it would be much more so for the uninformed man walking the street.

Like a shooting star in the night sky, the thought that I should write a book flashed into my mind. And with it also came the name of the book and the names of many of the chapters I should write about. After recording this information, as I tried to sleep waves of new ideas "flooded" my mind. And by four-thirty in the morning, a mere four and a half hours after this all started, the outline of a complete book had come to light.

I think I should add, I am not a writer—never have been, and my academic background is a scientific one. As a matter of fact, until now, it was always difficult for me to put my thoughts to paper. And that is why, as I mentioned before; I can't help but believe there is an unseen hand at work here.

I ask that you take a little journey with me. Maybe a route you're not accustomed to. But believe me, you'll arrive "unscathed," and just a little bit more informed.

Most travellers find a few scenes attractive along the way. If this "trip" is like that for you, then this book will have accomplished what it has set out to do.

Please understand, there is no attempt here, not in the least, to change your faith or belief in any way, shape, or form. All that is asked, is that you "travel" with an open mind; unbiased, and give a little thought to the ideas presented here.

CHAPTER 1 | The Search

Many years ago, a favourite expression of a hockey player I admired a lot was: "If it ain't broke, don't fix it!" Similarly, in man's life, when everything is "fun," health is good, prosperity "reigns," there is a happy family life, love is in the air, and everything is seen through rose-coloured glasses, it's not easy to change the status quo.

Let's turn to the past, some 2,500 years ago, where this scenario is "magnified" many times over, in what is now present-day Nepal. There lived a young prince named Siddhartha Gautama. Who from the very early days of childhood was prevented from leaving the palace precincts; so that he could not see the "miseries" that existed beyond the palace grounds. As his father only wanted him to be aware of his idyllic surroundings; filled with luxury and comfort, and that which was "good." And also to be cognizant of that he was used to—being of royal birth. One day, as "fate" would have it, he escaped from his "confinement" with his devoted charioteer. As they rode through the streets of the city, Gautama noticed a wrinkled, grey-haired man with bent frame passing by. Observing such a sight for the first time, he inquired of his rider, "What kind of man is this?"

To which his charioteer replied, "His are the symptoms of old age."

And Gautama was disturbed, as he wondered how people could be happy when eventually they became like this. As he and his charioteer moved on, there at the wayside, Gautama saw a crippled man, groaning as he laid on the pavement. Again Gautama asked, "What is the cause of his suffering?"

And his escort said, "This is sickness, which befalls all men."

Shocked again! at such a gruesome sight, a shudder went through Gautama's spine; to think that this could one day, befall him too. Continuing ahead, they encountered a crowd of people carrying a motionless body in a "box," wailing as they went. Again, Gautama inquired, "What is it they carry?"

And his charioteer told him: "This is a funeral procession on its way to the crematory grounds, as there is no life in the body!"

On hearing this and learning that all men shared this fate, Gautama's views on life underwent a sudden and dramatic change. He realized for the first time that the glory of life was evanescent; like a puff of smoke in the wind. But at the same time, these experiences awakened the latent compassion in his heart, for the suffering of humanity.

Returning home, he had a farewell peek at his sleeping wife and son. Then, with a bowl and a simple robe, he departed the palace grounds, in his search for truth—which would free mankind forever from sorrow and suffering. And which would give him complete understanding of the mystery of life and death. Truth which he did find! and henceforth he became known as the "Enlightened One"—the Buddha.

This story reminds us of the impermanence of the seemingly happy lives we are currently living. And although things may not be "broke," it should make us wonder, that if a prince and future king could renounce everything to find the meaning of life, what about us? Shouldn't we be a little more piqued in our interest—in trying to unravel the mysteries of life, too?

PARAMAHANSA YOGANANDA[1]

As a youngster growing up in India, Yogi Paramahansa's mother—Gurru Ghosh, was his pride and joy. And to say she was the dearest thing to him in the world is an understatement. Her kindness, understanding, caring, and selflessness were matchless.

A funny incident with regards to her endearing nature occurred one day, when Gurru Ma[2] packed her things, called a cab, and planned to leave home in a rush. All because she had been mildly rebuked by her husband for spending more on feeding the poor in one fortnight, than he had earned in a month. (Although, she did change her mind, after a little coaxing from him).

"Mother" was a God-fearing and very devotional woman; and she had played a big part in her son's strong religious upbringing. She was the one who introduced him to the Indian spiritual epics—the Ramayana and the Bhagavad Gita. And many a day found them in meditation together; enjoying the inner peace of deep spiritual communion, as well as the pleasure of each other's company.

So, when Gurru Ghosh unexpectedly passed away, it's easy to see why Mukunda[3] wanted to end it all—there and then, by throwing himself in front of an oncoming train.

It is at this point in his life, even though he was just eleven years old, that he began his search for a healing for his unbearable pain. Although his journey did have its ups and downs, he finally did meet his guru, who helped him to attain self-realization—which proved to be the panacea to all of his ailments.

The essence of this story is that trials and tribulations are not "enemies," which are meant to torment us. But like ore that is purified in the furnace, pain purges us and prepares us for advancement on the spiritual path.

---

1 Author of many spiritual books, including *Autobiography of a Yogi;* founder of Self-Realization Fellowship in Los Angeles, California; and also my beloved guru.

2 A title of respect meaning mother.

3 The master's Christian name, before being bestowed with the holy title: Paramahansa.

Just like a weary bird flying over the vast ocean knows its sole refuge is the mast of the solitary ship, sailing below. It is only when man is burdened with extremely trying circumstances, that he realizes his sole source of comfort, is turning —to a Higher Power.

TYPES OF MEN SEEKING THE DIVINE

Lord Krishna says in the Bhagavad Gita: Along with the seekers of truth (Gautama), and those undergoing trials and tribulations (Sri Yogananda); there are two other classes of "men" who become his devotees, (which is the same as becoming a devotee of his bona fide spiritual teachers):

> Persons who are initially drawn to the presence of spiritual masters, because they may have heard, or read, about their supernormal powers. (Which should come as no surprise, as we all know, man has always been in awe of the extraordinary. After all, didn't Christ say, "Except ye see signs and wonders, ye will not believe."?)[4]

> And those interested, in attaining wealth.[5]

That is why we find self-realized masters perform miracles; first to attract the attention of the masses—then they can impart to them what they are really here to give; namely, spiritual truths—which ultimately lead to enlightenment!

HIDDEN MEANING IN THE PARABLE OF THE SOWER

Of course, not all are persuaded to change their worldly lives, after hearing about life's great mysteries! As is made clear by the parable of the sower, as taught by Jesus, which says: A sower went out to sow seeds,

---

4   John 4:48
5   VII:16.

and as he sowed they fell in different places: some by the wayside, and the birds came and devoured them; some on stony ground, which sprouted very quickly, but lacking strong roots, soon withered under the sun's rays; a few among thorns, and the thorns sprung up, and choked them; and the rest on good ground, which produced an abundance of fruit.[6] The interpretation[7] being: When illumined masters give their sermons, man can only "receive" according to his readiness; the good ground representing the "ready" ones, who can easily assimilate and put into practice what is being preached to them. (The first, second and third scenarios represent those with closed minds, who cannot appreciate what they hear; those who get emotionally worked up at first and soon lose interest; and those who have so many irons in the fire that spiritual matters get crowded out of their agendas, respectively.)

This is again reinforced by Jesus, when he was asked by his disciples, "Why speakest thou unto them [the masses] in parables."

To which he replied, "Because it is given unto you to know the mysteries of the kingdom of heaven, but to them it is not given…Therefore speak I to them in parables, because they seeing see not; and hearing they hear not, neither do they understand."[8]

The interpretation[9] being: It was easy for the disciples to understand the mysteries of heaven, because they lived a spiritual life and strictly adhered to their teacher's (Jesus') precepts. Whereas the populace, with their indifference to spiritual teachings and to walking the spiritual path, were incapable of understanding and putting into practice what they heard and saw. Nevertheless, by the use of parables, each man is able to "receive" and put into practice, according to their level of understanding. Thus, at least, enabling some to progress on the spiritual path.

---

6   Matthew 13:1-9 and 18-23
7   Interpretation from: The Daily Study Bible: The Gospel of Matthew; Volume 2, Chapters 11-28 (Revised Edition) by William Barclay. Ontario, Canada: G.R. Welch Co. Ltd; 1975. Pages 59-61.
8   Matthew 13:10,11,13.
9   Explanation from: The Yoga of Jesus by Paramahansa Yogananda. Los Angeles, California: Self-Realization Fellowship, 2009. Page 43.

MY OWN PATH

My path ... was not so much a search as an indirect guidance to what is real and what is illusory, and it unfolded in different steps as the years rolled by.

I was born into a Moslem home, and like the apple which doesn't fall far from the tree, this is the faith I practiced in my formative years. (And at that time, that seemed the right thing to do.) Not to any extreme, but something that give me guidance to be able to differentiate between what is considered good and what is considered sinful. I never really read the Koran, but occasionally I went to the mosque, on special days of prayer and celebrations. And sometimes during the holy month of Ramadan, I made a determined effort and fasted.

But from an early period in my life, (before I was a teenager), there were certain things that I found I didn't like about myself. It dawned on me that I wasn't as confident as I wanted to be. I wondered what it would be like to have control of my thoughts, as they always seemed to be rushing into my mind in an endless stream; like countless tributaries flowing into the ocean. And I think, maybe, I even had an inferiority complex. Then one day, it suddenly crossed my mind; this was the way I'd come into the world, and this was the way I was going to leave it. Not too reassuring, in the least!

In my early teens, my parents took me on a trip to New York City. (I am the only offspring, and I was lucky to be taken on many overseas trips when I was still a youngster.) And one day, while we were shopping in a very huge and busy department store, my mother told me to remain in a corner while she and my father looked around. As it turned out, I was standing directly next to a rotating rack, filled with an array of books. To pass the time away, I spun the rack to look at the fancy designs on the covers, with no interest as to what might be inside—(as at that time, I really didn't have a passion for reading, as yet). When, the big bold letters—"YOGA," written across one of the covers, suddenly caught my attention. Up to that time, I had never heard or even seen the word yoga before. But like a long-lost friend, it seemed quite familiar to me. As a matter of fact, as I write, I still can see as clearly as if it were yesterday, the cover with the bright red background, and a woman sitting in a contorted hatha yoga[10] posture, in the foreground. Turning to the back cover, I was intrigued to learn that the practice of yoga is conducive to peace of mind, and among other things, also helps with the improvement of one's self-confidence. This really got my attention, and I envisioned I might be lucky not to leave the world, "the same way," as I had entered it. So, I bought the book, and without knowing it at the time, this was the beginning of my journey. It had nothing to do with spirituality, but it gave me great hopes of becoming someone whom I would rather be!

This was my introduction to meditation, and along with that, I also learned some hatha yoga and breathing exercises.

Although there were some benefits to what I was doing, I did not get the results I was so eagerly anticipating. As it never occurred to me it would take more than a casual approach, and it required a lot more discipline and steadfastness to accomplish what the book had "promised."

At around the same period in my life, I started reading many books written by a Tibetan lama—T. Lobsang Rampa, which describe his exceptional life and experiences in a monastery—(including *The Third Eye*), which for a youngster, was quite a "mind-blowing" revelation. But more importantly, his explication of matters of an occult nature, gave me a nice background to complement my involvement with the practical side of things.

My familiarity with Rampa's discussion on subjects such as astral projection, silver cord, reincarnation, akashic records, and astral planes served me well, as I delved further into these teachings, later on in life.

---

10   A system of complex bodily postures (asanas), which facilitates physical well-being, as well as, has a calming effect on the mind.

A TREASURE TROVE OF SPIRITUAL WISDOM

Highly evolved spiritual men have walked the sacred land of India in many of the last centuries, as they do now. Even the renowned conqueror, Alexander the Great, was so impressed with the holy men, yogis, and ascetics he encountered when he invaded northwestern India in 327-325 B.C. that when he withdrew, he took with him his own spiritual guru—Kalyana, also known as Swami Sphines. (And for those who are passionate about the facts of history, it was Alexander who coined the oft much-misunderstood name—Hindus, for the natives residing on the banks of the Indus; which is a translation of the original name; Indoos—from his native tongue.)

But, as can be expected, it can be quite difficult and inconvenient for many to travel to a far-off land in pursuit of a guru. Who in many cases, can prove to be as elusive to find as a needle in a haystack; unless, of course, one knows beforehand about their whereabouts.

For those with a genuine thirst for truth, who are trying to unravel the mysteries of life, and who are basically just beginning on their spiritual journey, a good way to get started is to become a member of the Theosophical Society: the Holy Grail of literary works on the Ancient Spiritual Wisdom. Which shouldn't be a major issue, as its main prerequisite simply requires one to be involved in some activity contributing to the benefit of mankind.

This is not such a bad idea, as it is wise to remember that from the initial stage of being inspired, (which is acquired from philosophical and theological research), one moves up the spiritual ladder, to being filled with aspiration, and from here, one is elevated even further; one's desire intensifying strongly, to a point where one wants to become self-realized.

The headquarters is located in Adyar, Chennai, in the state of Tamil Nadu, India. Where it has been since 1882, after relocating from Bombay[11] in 1878; (but originating in New York, in 1875). Nevertheless,

---

11   Renamed Mumbai since 1995.

there are many branches (lodges), which can be found dotted throughout the globe.

The essence of their teachings is based on the underlying oneness of everything that exists, (both the animate and the inanimate); in essence, the truth that forms the underlying core of all the great religions. However, members are allowed to form their own opinions and draw their own conclusions, as the Society does not advocate adherence to any of its teachings.

The founders of this sacred institution, which is said to be "looked over" by the mahatmas,[12] were Madame Blavatsky and Colonel H.S. Olcott. The former became much more of a household name, though, as she was a world-renowned author and was also well known for performing feats of a miraculous nature!

It is interesting to note that an illumined master at the time—Ramalinga Swami, prophesied the coming of these two great "founders." His prediction read: "With their coming, the ancient Eastern spiritual teachings would be more readily accepted by the people of the West; because these teachers would also come from here."

It is not unusual for people studying at the headquarters to be so "moved" by the teachings that they eagerly head out in search of spiritual gurus, so that they can put into practice what they just learned in theory.

For those interested in a less formal approach, there are many books written by gurus or their disciples touting their master's teachings. In the past, finding such books may have posed a problem, but now, with the internet, the information is just a mouse click away.

Nevertheless, how you're led to your path, is another story.

In conclusion: here is a little poem, that sums it all up.

---

12   Great souls; men of God-realization.

OUR SEARCH

Our search begins when
We realize the transiency of life;
Our search begins
When we are empty inside.
Our search begins when
Our pain is too hard to bear;
Our search begins when
A craving is near.
Our search begins when
It is destined to be;
Which is the same as,
I hear an inner call,
Beckoning to me!

CHAPTER 2 | # Fate or Coincidence

 A lot of music lovers from the older generation who followed rock and roll music should know about "The Day the Music Died"—famous lyrics from the hit, "American Pie" by Don McLean. The phrase refers to the tragic accident on February 3, 1959, which took the lives of the much beloved musicians, "The Big Bopper" Richardson, Buddy Holly, and Ritchie Valens.

If we look at all the unusual events leading up to this incident, making a case that this was fate as opposed to coincidence seems more logical than not. In doing so, we should bear in mind, too, that timing is a factor in the equation that determines the outcome in these scenarios.

From the inception of the Winter Dance Party tour that the musicians were on at the time, it definitely seemed that the bus they took wasn't the greatest idea. Especially considering the extensive mileage between venues, travelling through the very thick snow, when the bus kept breaking down. And when the heating in the vehicle did the same, it certainly seemed like an ominous sign, as it was in the middle of winter and extremely cold outside.

Evidently then, from this early stage on the tour, the mind-set of the group involved was no doubt already going through some changes.

Which, inevitably, would have affected how they made their decisions, later on.

At this point, another scene of the drama had already unfolded, as one of the "players," Carol Bunch, (Buddy Holly's drummer), had contracted frost bite, due to the poor heating conditions on the bus, and had to be hospitalized.

Arriving in Clear Lake, Iowa, the performers did a gig at the Surf Ballroom, which was not part of their much-anticipated tour.

To make life a "little simpler," Buddy Holly decided to charter a plane for himself and his two backup musicians, so that they could travel in comfort to their next gig in Moorhead, Minnesota, avoid some of the major inconveniences of travelling by bus, and at the same time, have lots of time left, to do his "piled up" laundry.

And, so to speak, the "wheels" of what was to come were set into motion. "The Big Bopper" secured a seat on the plane, by replacing Waylon Jennings, (Holly's bass player), who had come down, with the flu, while Ritchie Valens "won" a seat by the flip of a coin with Tommy Allsup, (Holly's guitarist). And finally, Dion DiMucci (from Dion and the Belmonts), didn't even consider getting on board, as he thought that the thirty-six-dollar fare was a little too steep for his taste. His decision was so trivial, it's hard to conceive! As obtaining the money would have been the least of his problems—maybe it was his "inner voice" guiding him, since not being one of the passengers actually saved his life.

Taking a look at the big picture, it looked like a "game" of musical chairs, and when the "music died," there was no one to occupy the last seat. As the plane crashed soon after takeoff. How strange! that so many unusual circumstances came together in such a short period of time, to create a tragedy of such historic proportions.

It should be added, too, that if the timing to the build-up of events had been different, it is possible that another pilot might have been at the controls. And maybe, the outcome of the scenario would have been different. As it was later determined, that the cause of the accident was partly due to pilot error, along with poor weather conditions.

And lastly, it should be noted that although Buddy Holly was quite famous at the time, he was forced to hit the road again because of financial difficulties and just wanted to make some quick money.

So here again, we have to ponder—was it fate or coincidence, that Holly's dilemma coincided with the tour? Other questions we have to ask are—was his financial situation avoidable? (If yes! he wouldn't have been on the road), and was it really necessary for him to go on tour again, despite his financial crisis?

So, eerily enough, it looks almost like the plane was meant to take off. And as if the names of the passengers to be on board were already recorded by an invisible hand!

A PERSONAL EXPERIENCE

Leaving for work one day, several years ago, I was already halfway through the door, when it suddenly dawned on me that I should call a friend I hadn't spoken to in a while. So I retraced my steps and went to give him a call. This was quite unusual, though, as I don't spend a lot of time on the phone, and also, this was the first time I had ever called someone before leaving for work.

After a short chat with my friend, I was in my car headed to work, on a bright, sunny, winter's day. On my way, up ahead, I noticed a stationary car on a road to the right, trying to make a turn into the lane leading in the opposite direction.

It was around two o'clock in the afternoon, and at that exact moment, these were the only two vehicles on the scene.

Coming to a stop, about twelve feet in front of the car, (to allow the driver to turn), guess what? The driver headed straight into the front of my car. It wasn't fatal, but there was nevertheless considerable damage, and I thought to myself, *If I didn't change my mind when I was already halfway through the door, none of this would have happened.*

Here again is an example where timing was a factor in the turn of events. Because for the accident to occur, the two vehicles had to be at the same place at the same time. Hence, what took place looks more like something that was meant to be, rather than just a random incident occurring.

MISSING THE JACKPOT

I personally know of two persons ("lottery lovers"), who have been playing the same numbers religiously every single week for many, many years, without ever winning a single penny. And just the one time they opted not to play—guess what? Their numbers came in. There had been more than ample time for them to get their tickets before closing time. But being preoccupied with trivial matters, they had decided against it, as they figured they never won anything, anyway.

Imagine that! The one time they missed, their numbers came in. And they could have been millionaires. Now! Is that fate, or is it merely a case of eerie coincidence?

In life, situations like these are occurring around us all the time. But unless we have directly experienced them, or they have played a part in the lives of those around us, it is difficult to see whether it's fate at play, or just random events occurring.

However, when one has a genuine thirst for spiritual growth, one is able to distinctly discern that the circumstances that unfold with regards to one's progress are no mere accidents but are, in fact, a series of pre-determined events, helping one on one's spiritual journey. Albeit, one doesn't recognize them exactly at the time that they are unfolding. And what better example to demonstrate this, than how it relates to my life?

MY NEW HOME

The year was 1972, and I came to Canada with my parents, who were trying to get me motivated, with regards to my studies. Although, after about eight months, they suddenly "folded tent," and returned home. But before they did, they "shopped" me around to see which of my aunts or uncles would keep me until I completed high school, (which would take another year). At which time I would begin attending university, (as the plan was for me to live on the campus). But as it turned out, there were no "takers," so I ended up residing with an older cousin and her family, who at the time I really didn't know that well, because she is quite a bit older than me, and naturally, our lives led in different directions. Needless to say, I was in the dark to these situations, until after the fact.

Reflecting on these circumstances later on in life, I realized that if it weren't for me ending up at this address, the possibility of my progressing on the spiritual path would have been almost an impossibility. As none of my family members, friends, or people around me, had any great interest in spirituality or enthusiasm to expand their religious beliefs, beyond the dogmas they were familiar with.

My cousin's brother-in-law, a very charismatic guy with the gift of gab, who is much older than me, also resided here. He was an avid reader, and although his field of interest was anthropology, (he later went on to get his PhD); he nevertheless had a great passion for philosophy and religion. To this end, he owned quite a remarkable collection of books on these subjects. For the first time in my life, I was able to become familiar with the in-depth teachings of the Buddha, was made aware of different forms of meditation, and most invaluably of all, I read *Autobiography of a Yogi* by Paramahansa Yogananda—who later became my guru. And I owe it all to my buddy—"Mr. Charismatic," for it was through his collection of books that this information became available to me.

This experience was all well and good, but I was not prompted to take my spiritual journey beyond the literary level, until the year 1975.

That year, while spending the summer at my cousin's home, (after returning from university), I ran into another "jewel"—a book on transcendental meditation, (or TM, as it is more commonly known). The technique had become a worldwide phenomenon in the sixties, when the Beatles and a group of friends headed to the Himalayan foothills to spend time with his holiness Maharishi Mahesh Yogi (the founder of the movement) at his ashram; in Rishikesh, India.

This book, which so captured my attention, was authored by four professionals from different backgrounds (including a psychiatrist and a philosopher), who wanted to share their personal experiences from meditating, as well as the findings of scientists on people who meditated. Findings that proved mesmerizing, as many experiments revealed TM produced spectacular benefits to its practitioners (confirmed by their own personal experiences). And it also had an overwhelmingly positive effect on the residents of those areas where people were practicing this form of meditation.

To say I was in awe of their findings is an understatement. And I was ready to run out and join the "club." However, without really doing much inquiring as to how to do so, I put the matter to rest, and my exuberance gradually subsided.

Several months later, I was back to my studies. And just the second day at classes, I was walking down the corridors headed to one of my lectures. And lo and behold, there, pinned up on one of the walls, I saw a large poster inviting one and all to an introductory lecture on transcendental meditation. Talk about opportunity knocking at your doorstep.

Needless to say, within the week I was a full initiate, and I became a dedicated practitioner for seven years—faithfully adhering to my practice of two twenty-minute sessions daily. Until I climbed the spiritual ladder a little higher, when I decided to be initiated into a technique that I consider to be far more advanced. But more on that later.

Something about how I was unknowingly placed in a foreign environment, surrounded by such a wealth of spiritual knowledge—giving me the foresight to realize that I would one day move up the spiritual ladder, made me reflect on a somewhat similar situation that happened to a very young, unassuming Franciscan friar, a long, long time ago, in the ancient town of Ancona, Italy.

While in the company of other monks, (having joined the order the day before), the friar unexpectedly crossed paths with a complete stranger, who immediately approached him and knelt at his feet. The other monks, inquiring about the strange incident that had just taken place, were told that the young man would become the next Pope of Rome!

The name of the unknown Franciscan friar was Felice Peretti, a former swine herder. And that of the stranger was no other than the incomparable seer—Michel de Nostradamus. (The prophesy was fulfilled in 1585, and Felice ruled as Pope Sixtus V, until the year 1590.)

MY LAST TRIP TO MY HOMELAND

During a return visit to Guyana in 1978, I had a unique experience while visiting at a friend's house one evening.

As we sat chatting in his living room, I couldn't help being mysteriously drawn to a life-sized, coloured photograph of someone I had never seen before, positioned directly across from where I was sitting. Although the moppy, Afro-type hairstyle was reminiscent of a young Michael Jackson, the other distinguishing feature was that this personage wore a full-length, saffron-coloured robe. It was hard to contain my curiosity for any length of time, and I finally had to inquire who the person was. Looking at me straight in the face, without even blinking an eye, my friend retorted, "That is God!"

I was so totally taken aback by his reply that I spontaneously started laughing uncontrollably, as I had never heard anything so preposterous before. So much so, that I needed a few tissues to wipe the water that was running from my eyes.

That was that, and I carried on the rest of the evening as though the conversation had never taken place.

For my remaining stay, of about six months in Guyana, never once did I reflect upon what had transpired that night, nor did I ever try to find out who the person in the photograph was.

RETURN TO CANADA

I had always enjoyed reading books, which contributed to my spiritual edification, but I should mention that reading such books had now become one of my favourite pastimes.

So once back in Canada, I visited a favourite haunt (the Fifth Kingdom bookstore), where I usually could find one of these hard-to-find "gems." It was a rather unique place and shouldn't even be referred to as a bookstore. It was just a small, insignificant-looking, square room, on the second floor of a house, with just a collection of a few hundred books. Nonetheless, it was probably the only place in Toronto where one could procure hard-to-find books on philosophy, religion, and metaphysical subjects.

On my first visit there, I had a pleasant surprise waiting for me. One of the first books I picked up, would you guess? There on the cover was the same person with the Afro hairstyle I had recently seen, in the picture in Guyana. The name of the book was *Sai Baba, Man of Miracles*, (Murphet 1973); and in an instant —the mystery as to whom the robed man was, was solved! A spiritual leader with millions of followers around the world. And revered as divinity in human form—an avatar![13]

With the purchase of Murphet's book, I went on to own fourteen other books on Baba's life and teachings. And thus began my lifelong devotion to this spiritual "Guru."

Some of the more colourful titles I have in my possession are: *When God Walks the Earth*, (Shemesh 1992); *Miracles Are My Visiting Cards*, (Erlendur Haraldsson 1987); and *God, Nature and Man*, (Antonio and Sylvie Craxie 1985).

Although I own a fine collection of books on Sai Baba, I think that's just the tip of the iceberg; as Sri Sathya Sai Baba is one of the most written-about personalities on the planet.

Interestingly enough, it should be noted too, that it was my good friend the anthropologist who introduced me to the bookstore. Hence it is obvious, he once again played a part in the unfolding of my spiritual path.

---

13   Descent of divinity into flesh: A soul that becomes one with Spirit while on earth; which then returns (if it wills) in a next incarnation, to help mankind do the same.

THE SACRED ASH

Just around the same time I started reading *Man of Miracles*, my wife Bibi (who was just a friend at the time), told me that she was experiencing a very strange phenomenon in her bedroom. Apparently, she said, it seemed as though particles of dust were continually falling from a small statue of Lord Shiva (one of the Gods of the Hindu trinity[14]), which was sitting atop her bedhead. She said that every morning she cleaned it up, but surprisingly, the next day there was always some more there, as though she had never done so.

The puzzling thing though, was that the room was small with only one window, which was always closed because it was winter. So how could dust enter the room?

All I could do was ask whether she had saved any of it.

She told me she had and produced some in a tissue, from her purse. And I was totally astounded to see it resembled something I had just read about the day before, in *Man of Miracles*—something called vibhutti; a sacred ash produced by Sai Baba by circling his downward-turned palm a few times, and then making a fist, to prevent it from falling to the ground.

This is considered a panacea and it is given to his devotees, who eat it, or apply it to the forehead (at the point of the spiritual eye), or on other body parts. (By the way, although this may sound strange to those hearing about the phenomenon for the first time, there are probably millions of people who have witnessed its manifestation, when "Baba walked the earth." When this miracle was performed, almost on a daily basis.) Now, returning to my story. After getting over my surprise, I had a taste of the ash, and then there was no doubt in my mind—that this was no earthly substance. As it was edible, had its own unique taste, and was quite pleasing to the palate.

---

14 The other two being: Brahma—the Creator and Vishnu—the Sustainer.

And so, that was my introduction to this otherworldly substance, and since then, I have been able to make use of its curative properties on many occasions—but that's another story.

Although I've had experiences like these in my life, I've had to keep them a secret. As one does not go around discussing such things, with any and everyone. Especially so, when they are not Hindus, or haven't a clue who Sai Baba is. Not to mention, they might even think you're a bit nuts!

In any event, blessings from the Divine are a personal thing—and that's all that matters.

BECOMING A DISCIPLE

In 1982, I became a disciple of Paramahansa's through his Self-Realization Fellowship headquarters, in Los Angeles, California.

This involved receiving biweekly lessons through the mail, which were a comprehensive edification on spiritual matters, and included initiation into very advanced spiritual techniques.

There is a probationary period of several months before one becomes eligible to receive initiation into Kriya yoga; the highest form of meditation taught by Self-Realization Fellowship. But seeing that I wasn't prepared to make the lifestyle changes that accompany initiation into such an advanced technique, I postponed my initiation until the year 1990.

A TRIP OF A LIFETIME

In much the same way as I started writing this book, I decided to go to India.

I had just finished my meditation one morning, sometime in the summer of 1992, and just like that, the thought hit me; *I am going to India —I am going to Sai Baba's ashram*[15]— Prasanthi Nilayam; in the small village of Puttaparthi, in southern India.

---

15   A spiritual hermitage.

The great irony in me deciding to do so, is that it had been impossible for me to believe that Sai Baba was divine when I'd first heard that he was an avatar. And there I was fourteen years later, planning to go to some extremely remote corner of the world, to be in his holy presence. The other unusual thing is—I am not very fond of travelling. Forget far-off places! I even dislike straying too far from home.

Apart from a few trips to Guyana in the seventies and a short visit to New York in the eighties —that's it! So when I add I was planning to make the trip alone, it is easy to grasp that this is not something I would normally do. Nevertheless, I had a pretty good idea where I was headed as I had read many stories of how people found their way there, and where they were able to secure suitable accommodations—not to mention owning a travel guide on India by *Lonely Planet*, was an invaluable tool in allowing me to put my itinerary together.

I left Canada on the evening of 19 February, 1993, and arrived at the ashram around two P.M. on 23 February. My original plan was to stay for two weeks, but I had to leave a day earlier, due to a severe bout of diarrhea. This simple deviation from my original plan proved to be a real blessing in disguise. As it saved me a lot of unnecessary worry, utter frustration, and probably even worse! in days to come.

Anyway, my stay there was everything I expected it to be, and more! The serene, spiritual atmosphere and the holy vibrations at the ashram proved to be quite beneficial to my daily meditations. But the most amazing thing was to be able to see the sacred ash—(vibhutti), being "produced" on a daily basis by Baba; by merely making a few horizontal, clockwise circles with his hand.

Who would have imagined that I would one day witness this incredible phenomenon right before my eyes, when I'd first read about it, fourteen years earlier? It surely makes one wonder whether this is just merely another case of coincidence!

Without going into all the details about my experiences at the ashram, I think I should nevertheless mention an incident that I found to be quite amusing.

One day, I was sitting in the open air, in the second row among the vast crowds. As Baba walked by, he stopped to collect a letter from an old Indian gentleman who was sitting in the front row, and to the left of me. As Swami stretched forward to collect the letter; I gently pushed myself up a little from the sitting position and held on to his right shoulder for several seconds. Hoping, (like the way the people in the times of Jesus did; to be cured of their ailments), I too would be healed of a pain in my lower left leg, which had been bothering me for a very long time, and which no doctor in the last ten years had been able to cure. (Something I'd contemplated doing even before leaving Canada, and which actually came to pass).

Although, I wasn't healed immediately. After a period of about three months, there was no trace of pain for me to complain about, and it has remained that way, ever since.

Despite being denied a personal interview, (something almost impossible to get, considering the massive crowds that are always present), Swami did accept my letter with a request for help, with regards to matters I found a little difficult resolving on my own.

Well! all good things come to an end. And I was back in Bangalore (which is about 110 miles from Puttaparthi), on Monday March 8; at the same hotel I'd stayed at before heading to the ashram.

The main purpose of my trip was accomplished, and with five days remaining I was just planning to take it easy and get lots of needed rest. But I still had to confirm my flight to Canada, out of Bombay, on the coming Saturday. Also, I was really looking forward to spending an extra night (Thursday), at the luxurious five-star hotel—the Airport Centaur in Bombay, added on to the approximately twelve hours from Friday evening to Saturday morning I had originally planned.

As a matter of fact, it had been my intention to kill a few hours there, on my arrival to India. But the unreasonable rate of $105.00 U.S., they quoted me for my fourteen-hour layover in Bombay, didn't seem justifiable. Instead, I used the few hours to go sight-seeing, which as it turned out, was a far wiser choice.

This time, however, money wasn't an issue, as I had lots of spare cash, due to spending so little in Puttaparthi. Nevertheless, the only reason for singling out this hotel is its convenience; being just across from the domestic airport.

On Tuesday, I made several calls to the Air India office to confirm my flight out of Bombay, but it was impossible to get through, because the line was continually busy. After trying a few times the next morning, I was relieved to finally get an answer. But that was short-lived, as the first thing I was told was that the flight division of Air India was on strike, and that I should come down immediately, so that alternate arrangements could be made.

Having arrived at the office a little later on, the first thing I noticed was a long line of very nervous-looking people, some of whom, I had met at the ashram. And I couldn't contain my exuberance when they told me that Baba had left on Tuesday and was also in Bangalore. (I guess I had planned my stay at the ashram perfectly, as if it hadn't been for my illness, that's the exact day I would have left too.) But my exuberance didn't last long either. Because, after issuing me a temporary ticket to travel with British Airways, the travel agent couldn't get my flight confirmed when she called their office. As the computers were down, due to a temporary blackout.

I personally went down to the British Airways office, a little later on, but there was no change in the situation, so I was told to call them later on in the evening, before they closed.

So with nothing to do till then, I took a taxi and dashed off to Baba's estate at Whitefield, which was just about fifteen miles away.

The crowd wasn't as big, nor was the wait as long, as at Puttaparthi. And it wasn't long before Baba appeared. It was a cozy, intimate setting, which made it easier to feel his love and warmth. And one couldn't help getting the feeling that he was always watching over us. Once again, I was very lucky to get a close-up look at him materializing vibhutti. But I only stayed for a short while, as I had very important matters to take care of. And that was the last time I was blessed to be in his holy presence.

I returned to the hotel around 6:45 and called British Airways. The good news was that the computers were up and running, but my troubles were far from over. I was now told that I was a passenger on a waiting list, and that I should call the next morning for an update.

For a few hours the next morning, I had a problem getting through. When I finally did, I was told that nothing had changed; I was still on the waiting list, and I should come in Friday morning to make arrangements for an alternative flight; leaving on Monday... which would cost me, $1,000.00 U.S.

Needless to say, I became very despondent, as I realized I could be stuck —God knows for how long!

As is obvious, all previous plans for staying at the Centaur Hotel had to be forgone, as everything on my itinerary was now topsy-turvy.

Bright and early the next day, I arrived at the British Airways office. As I sat in front of the agent's desk, I couldn't help but noticing that she was deftly punching away at her computer keys—like a maestro at his piano. And continued to do so, for another fifteen minutes, which seemed quite unusual for someone just trying to print a ticket. However, when she finally spoke, it was like sweet music to my ears as she said I was now confirmed to fly out early Saturday morning from Bombay, on the standby flight, instead. But everything was far from being resolved. I was told I had several loose ends to tie up, before my flight could be confirmed. (There was so much to be done, and so little time to do it in!)

It was almost noon, and my first order of business was to head over to the Air India office, to get my original ticket reissued. Showing two stages of my flight from India, that is; Bombay to London, and London to Toronto. (Instead of one continuous trip, shown on my original ticket).

Then I had to hurry down to the Indian Airlines office, as I had to get my original departure time out of Bangalore changed from 8.00 P.M., to 4.00 P.M.

And if that weren't enough, I had to return to the British Airways office, to pick up my travel documents and confirmation.

(Not to mention, having fully expected to travel on Monday, I hadn't even begun to pack).

That's when very unusual things started happening. All at the Air India office, where I had headed down to in a big hurry. While I was waiting for my new ticket to be printed (showing the two stages of my journey), the computer "froze up," so I had to sit for another hour before the task could be completed. (Wasting precious time, which I already didn't have much of.) During this time, someone from the Indian Airlines office rang about a business matter. And the agent looking after me asked if it was possible to change my departure time (out of Bangalore) without me having to go there. This was done! Next, someone from the British Airways office called with regards to another issue and was asked if they could be so kind as to fax my travel documents. That was done! —and just like that all my loose ends came together, without even having to step one foot out of the building.

In writing about all this confusion that took place in the last days of my trip, I couldn't help getting a feeling of déjà vu. As it reminded me so much of how things kept bizarrely switching around before Buddy Holly and his fellow musicians boarded the plane, on that fateful day— "The Music Died."

Arriving safely in Bombay, I was relieved to be rid of all the confusion. At least, I could relax in comfort now, if I could spend my last few hours (which I had so been looking forward to), at the more accommodating Centaur Hotel.

So I jumped into a taxi and told the driver to take me there. Without giving me a clue as to his response, he said, "The hotel was bombed, just a little while ago. Several people were killed, and many more injured."

Like hail falling from a sunny sky, I immediately went from being completely at ease, to being numb all over, and becoming speechless. But then again, I started thinking, *Well! At least I'm alive!* Not only had the hotel been bombed; but within a span of three hours, from 1:30 to 4:30 P.M., twelve other bombs went off in the vicinity, leaving in their wake, two hundred and fifty dead, and a far greater number wounded. Making it the worst wave of criminal violence in the country's history.

And if it weren't for all the unusual events preventing me from sticking to my original itinerary, I would have been at this exact place, at this exact time.

It should be noted, that the only reason for including the events of the last five days of my trip is their relevance to the theme of the chapter. And as they say: What's a story, without a happy ending?

With regards to the episodes of my spiritual journey, it is obvious that each step was always slow in the coming; albeit always moving forward. But the big question is: Were they just a matter of coincidences—or were they already written in the stars?

THE JOURNEY

It's worrisome to think,
That if the journey of life
Were a million steps to climb;
A far way yes!
Hard to picture in
The mind—
Yet! reality stands
The test of time.
What a pity! for those
Who don't even know
The ladder exists.
Surely somehow
A time will come;
When to solve
The mystery of life,
Will become, too hard
To resist!

CHAPTER 3 | Karma

 A lot more people are now familiar with, and more or less have an idea what the word karma means, than a decade or two ago. But above and beyond that, they haven't really given the concept much thought, or tried to fully comprehend what it really means.

And for some, it is just a mystical "teaching," associated with the holy texts of Eastern religions—where it is expounded as a clear and profound truth.

The word karma comes from the Sanskrit kri; to do, and its meaning being; the "repayment" of an action in like form—action and reaction; whether it be good or bad. Or, simply put, it is the law of cause and effect, or what goes around comes around; the effects of which follow one, from life to life.

As the renowned American philosopher Emerson puts it, "The world looks like a mathematical equation, which, turn it how you will, balances itself. Every secret is told, every crime is punished, every virtue rewarded, every wrong redressed, in silence and certainty."[16]

In this respect, it is obvious that every human being becomes the moulder of his own destiny. And recognizing this as the law of justice, he should blame no one, or hold them responsible, for his fate in life. For

---

16   From Emerson's essay "Compensation"—included in his book *Essays*, first published in 1841.

life is like a game where the eventual outcome rests in how we choose to play our parts!

Some religions, despite not teaching about karma, give us a reminder of the concept in much subtler ways. (Although, it is not really the same, exact thing.) This being; if a person performs good and unselfish deeds—being a good Samaritan, when he dies, he goes to the astral paradise—Heaven; and vice versa. Indicating that doing good brings about a good "result." And doing bad, having the opposite effect. The stress always being in the doing of good. As depicted by Jesus' words, "Do unto others as you would have others do unto you."[17]

Apart from Eastern doctrines, though, the Bible tells us; "As you sow so shall you reap."[18] It's hard to see how there could be any ambiguity in the meaning of such a straight-forward, self-explanatory pronouncement. And although these words were used by the Apostle Paul, it's as though they were spoken by Jesus himself. As there is no doubt Paul would have gotten them from Christ's teachings.

Also, one may wonder what Jesus meant when he said, "For all they that take the sword shall perish with the sword."[19] Here again, this explicitly seems to say: evil begets evil. You hurt someone; you will be repaid in like manner. And from such a saying, one has to surmise that the opposite holds true too; good brings about good—which is exactly what karma means.

If there are still lingering doubts that the law of karma is indeed in the Bible, maybe then, these two other quotes should help to convince you. "Whoso sheddeth man's blood, by man shall his blood be shed."[20] And: "With the same measure that ye mete, it shall be measured to you."[21]

So, karma might not be a limiting principle after all, but instead, a universal truth!

---

17   Matt.7:12.
18   Galatians 6:7.
19   Matt. 26:52.
20   Genesis 9:6.
21   Luke 6:38.

In the material world, everything is based on duality, or the world of opposites. For example; good—bad, rich—poor, sickness—health; including as we all know, man's most treasured "possession"—his life; and its opposite—death. Therefore, isn't it highly illogical to think that something of far much lesser significance—his actions, would be the only exception to the rule (and not have their opposites—reactions), to this absolute "rule?" Wouldn't it?

If one believes in a just, caring, and loving Divine Being, isn't it a bit baffling, how come, not all men are created equal? Doesn't one wonder, why some people come into the world strong and healthy, and some are born with silver spoons in their mouths, while others are crippled, blind, deaf, deformed, sickly, or orphaned? Yet others are condemned to lives of utter poverty, where each and every day becomes a struggle for survival, with thousands dying daily, because they are unable to get a proper and timely meal, due to their unfortunate condition in life.

Well! If it isn't God's fault. Whose is it? The answer is: obviously our own—a payback for past actions. It may be a hard pill to swallow for some; but there is no other explanation. We are only reaping, what we have sown!

If viewed from another angle—isn't it puzzling why babies come into the world and without seemingly accomplishing one single thing, or not even getting a chance to "taste" what life is all about, their innocent lives are whisked away in a flash, hardly leaving a trace that they were ever even here?

Well! It's because, there was just a little karma for them to work out, and with that accomplished, the purpose of them being here was fulfilled—so they moved on.

So what may appear on the surface as a cruel injustice actually has a much deeper and meaningful underlying significance.

After all, doesn't the Bible tell us, "To everything there is a season, and a time to every purpose under the heaven: A time to be born, and a time to die..."[22]

Evidently from what is stated here there must be a purpose, even for those who are taken away after only a day, a week, or a month. And as mentioned before, that purpose can only be meaningful if viewed from a karmic point of view.

THE STORY OF KING DASARATHA

The effect of karma can rear its unsuspecting head, even in one lifetime. Even without us having a clue as to its influences in our everyday lives.

It doesn't necessarily take lifetimes before it surfaces with its iron-clad law of recurring retribution, as depicted by this tale from one of the great Indian spiritual classics—the Ramayana.

A long time ago, in the ancient kingdom of Kosala, the ruler, King Dasaratha, was forced to banish the apple of his eye—his son, Lord Rama; to the Dandaka forest for fourteen years where he had to live his life as an ascetic.

But the most dramatic part of this tale of separation is that it took place on the most auspicious day of his life—the day he was supposed to be coronated, as the king of Kosala.

King Dasaratha was forced to make this heartbreaking decision, as a result of having granted his youngest and favourite wife—Kaikeyi, two boons, for having nursed him back to health, after being seriously injured in battle, many years ago.

And on the eve of the coronation, Kaikeyi was reminded of these boons, by her scheming and conniving maid —Manthara. Who repeatedly prodded Kaikeyi into asking the king that her son Bharata be crowned king. (Rama being the son of Kausalya, the king's eldest of three wives). And secondly: "That Rama be banished to the forest, for fourteen years."

---

22   Ecclesiastes 3:1,2.

Although these actions would have been the last things to cross Dasaratha's mind; monarchs at that time lived by the law of dharma (that is, upholding the laws of truth and righteousness). So when Kaikeyi approached him, he had no choice but to acquiesce to her request. For to go against one's word was considered to be even worse than the fate of death.

With the departure of Lord Rama to the forest, the king's life became a living nightmare. Slowly and surely his strength ebbed from his once sturdy body.

But through his pain and agony, he could not fathom how such a cruel and unjust fate, could befall him.

Then it dawned on him—that it was retribution for a grievous deed he had heedlessly committed when he was but a young prince.

While hunting one day in a forest, the king had unwittingly taken the life of a young ascetic, whom he shot with an arrow, mistaking him, for his prey. Before dying, the ascetic requested that the king go at once to his ashram and inform his blind and elderly parents (whom he cared for), what he had done.

On hearing the tragic news, the aged couple were inconsolable. When the father was able to speak (after some introductory words), he said: "I curse you! that you too will suffer the same fate as I. You will also die! from the agony caused by separation, from your son."

And before the week was through, Dasaratha had reaped what he had sown. He died of a broken heart, during his sleep without ever seeing his beloved Rama, again.

A RARE GLIMPSE INTO PAST LIFE, AND ITS KARMIC EFFECTS IN THE NEXT

Unlike the previous tale, it is almost impossible to detect how karma may play out from a previous incarnation in the current one, (even to those who believe in many lives). The untrained mind is not that powerful a faculty, to go back that far in time!

In Phyllis Krystal's book: *Sai Baba The Ultimate Experience*[23] she describes a reverie she fell into one day, at her home in California. Her vocation involved working in reveries; helping others to resolve their problems, and in which her divine guru Baba assured her, he was always present; assisting and guiding her. But to which, she still had her misgivings.

In this session, Baba immediately appeared and requested that she follow him, as he casually walked through the vast crowds at his ashram, in Puttaparthi. He then quite suddenly stopped in front of a couple; a mother and her severely physically handicapped son (whom no doubt the mother had brought to be healed by Baba). Baba then asked Phyllis whether he should heal the boy or not. To which she readily and happily replied in the affirmative.

Again Baba motioned for her to follow him. This time, they were moving very rapidly through the air. After a while, it seemed that they had arrived at a place, somewhere back in time, where a judge was busy handing out sentences to offenders. Excepting that, it was quite obvious, the sentences were much too severe for the crimes that were committed. And the judge's overzealous assistant was taking great pride in his job, as well as seeming to be having great fun, as he recorded the sentences that were meted out, on a tablet.

Then Baba turned to Phyllis, to make sure she fully understood, what the scene depicted.

Incredibly, the two men were no other than the mother and child, she'd encountered, before the journey began. The judge was now the helpless, distorted, badly handicapped boy, and the mother was the lawyer's assistant, who through caring for her severely deformed son, was forced to learn the traits of love and compassion.

When they arrived back at Puttaparthi, Baba once again inquired whether Phyllis still wanted him to heal the child. This time, however, fully comprehending the situation, she unhesitatingly gave a negative answer.

---

23   Andhra Pradesh, India: Sri Sathya Sai Books and Publications Trust, 1985. Pages 241-243.

Several months later, when Phyllis was in India, seated among the large crowd at Baba's estate in Whitefield, she was quite enjoying the scene; watching Baba moving among his followers, taking their letters, blessing them, and now and then stopping to give advice to some very fortunate devotee, when for no apparent reason, he suddenly seemed to stand still. When Phyllis discerned the reason for his abrupt halt, she was absolutely flabbergasted. As he was standing right next to a mother and child, who were the exact replicas of the two persons she had envisioned in her reverie.

Although the experience was mainly to show that Baba was indeed present with her, during her work, and that it was not really her imagination playing tricks with her, it allows us to take a closer look as to why there are so many unexplained and hard to comprehend differences in the world.

FATE CAN BE CHEATED

The boomeranging effects of negative karma are not always written in stone. Simply put, circumstances are not made for man. But just the opposite—man is made for circumstances!

And so the possibility does exist that what is decreed by fate can also be altered.

However, (as we all know), if a colossal obstacle has to be removed, it simply cannot be done by a weak show of force. It can only be accomplished by tremendous faith and a super-strong will.

After all, Jesus attested to this fact when he proclaimed to his disciples; "Verily I say unto you, if ye have faith, and doubt not… if ye shall say unto this mountain, be thou removed and be thou cast into the sea; it shall be done."[24]

The adverse effects of karma can also be nullified or lightened through God's grace, by steady, intense, and sincere prayers.

---

24   Matt. 21:21.

Although, what may appear to be quite simple, may be much harder to accomplish, than what we might first expect.

As it is quite common, when we're broadcasting SOS, to have a lot more going on in our minds, than just our mere pleas for help.

And herein lies the problem; as our prayerful attempts can be compared to a transmission, being affected by a lot of static. Which prevents the "message" from being clearly received; not going through in an undistorted way, as it is supposed to.

Or viewed from another angle; our prayers usually lack the fire of devotion, to warm the heart of the "Petitioned."

Although it may seem farfetched, God-realized masters can also minimize, or totally negate, the painful and life-threatening effects that their very close disciples are supposed to go through, due to their "unfavourable" karma.

In *Autobiography of a Yogi*, Guruji describes how the deathless Babaji prevented his disciple from being burnt to bits, by taking on his karma and altering the outcome of his fate. Which the disciple would have had to experience, due to the effects of an unrighteous act, done in the past.

It occurred while the master and his close disciples were gathered around a huge fire that was lit for a Vedic ceremony. When for no apparent reason, Babaji pulled an ember from the ceremonial fire, and branded the bare shoulder of a disciple sitting nearby. When another disciple, also sitting nearby, inquired how could he do something so cruel, Babaji then calmly replied, "At this very moment, (according to his karma); this ill-fated disciple was supposed to have died, by being consumed in flames. But by 'taking on' his karma, and just allowing him to endure a fraction of what was decreed by faith—his life has now been spared." Then placing his healing hands on the disciple's badly burnt shoulder, Babaji made him "whole again!"[25]

---

25   Los Angeles, California: *Self-Realization Fellowship*, 2010. Thirteenth edition 1998. (First published in 1946). Excerpt from chapter 33: pages 335 and 336.

Another fascinating case involving a somewhat similar feat, where a devotee's life was spared, also took place in India around the early 1920s, in the port city of Mangalore.

In this instance, a great spiritual master, Swami Nityananda, (whose foremost disciple—Muktananda, became much more world renowned, due to his authorship of the spiritual classic: *Play of Consciousness*), performed the superhuman feat. Albeit, in a much more puzzling and mysterious way.

It occurred while the master was visiting at the home of a very close devotee. While she was cooking, Nityananda for no apparent reason, took an ember from the hearth, and struck her on the head with it. Then he unconcernedly exited the home, as though nothing had happened.

Obviously, the devotee's family was very infuriated and wanted to get their revenge. Nonetheless, the mother pacified them, probably knowing "deep down" that the master, who never harmed anyone, and who always had the welfare of his devotees at heart, had a very good reason for his strange and unusual behaviour, which was not quite obvious to them, yet!

A year later, a renowned astrologer was invited to give a family reading. To his utter amazement, he could not believe the woman was still alive. As there was every indication on the astrological charts, that she was supposed to have died, or become very ill, (with no possibility of recovery) at about the same time, she'd received the blow to the head.

Then it became clear to one and all that the blow must have somehow mitigated the effects of the destined tragedy.[26]

But probably the most publicized and documented case of the phenomenon is one regarding, Sri Sathya Sai Baba.

It took place at his ashram, in Puttaparthi, in 1963; just days before the great celebration of Guru Poornima day. A time when thousands gathered to hear Baba speak, get his blessings, and hopefully be entertained by a miracle or two.

---

26 From *Nityananda, the Divine Presence* by M. U. Hatengdi, page 43. Massachusetts: Rudra Press, 1984.

After informing a close aide he would no longer be giving interviews a few days before the festival, without the slightest symptom of being ill, Sri Sathya Sai Baba fell unconscious the following day.

He became very ill, with an extremely high fever, and within the next five days he suffered a severe stroke, and four massive heart attacks. His entire left side was paralyzed, and his speech and eyesight were also badly affected.

However, he said after the fifth day, his condition would not worsen. And that the distant devotee whose karma he had taken on (and who would have certainly died) had he not intervened to save his life and prevent his serious suffering, would be saved.

Then on the evening of the seventh day, (Guru Poornima day), after being assisted to his chair on the dais, before the great gathering. He asked that some water be brought, which was held close to his contorted lips, (also due to the stroke).

After taking a few sips, he dipped his fingers into the water, and sprinkled a few drops onto his paralyzed left arm and leg. Then he gently passed his right hand a few times over the affected areas. And in what must have been a magical moment for the audience to behold, he instantaneously healed himself!

And not only did he appear normal, as though he were never ill at all. But he carried on with his lengthy discourse as he usually did on these auspicious occasions and he led the crowd in the singing of holy songs (bhajans) and unlike when he first arrived, he made his way back to his room, up a long flight of stairs, unassisted![27]

For a law as "stiffly" set as karma, it is surely reassuring to learn from Lord Krishna: "Even if one commits the most abominable action, if he is engaged in devotional service (to Him, or any other form of Divinity), he

---

27   Recorded in *Sai Baba, The Holy Man and the Psychiatrist* by Samuel H. Sandweiss, pages 97-99. California, U.S.A.: Birth Day Publishing Company, 1975.

is to be considered saintly. He quickly becomes righteous, attains lasting peace, ... and he never perishes."[28]

And even if we are apt to lose hope, facing fate's cruel challenges, it is prudent to remember ultimately, (as already mentioned in chapter one), it's all a very subtle process of making us more spiritually purified.

---

28   Bhagavad Gita IX:30, 31.

KARMA

Karma, it's fair to say
Isn't really that easy to accept,
When no one knows for sure,
Why trials and tribulations are met?

It might appear as though
Things happen haphazardly.
But the good books say,
It's all—part of destiny.

Whatever man does,
Whether good or bad.
Will someday surely,
Make him happy or sad.

For the inexorable law of karma
Has a boomeranging effect.
Every action performed
Although not immediately realized;
Eventually returns to the doer.
Who has no choice;
But to trustingly accept!

CHAPTER 4 | Reincarnation

 As a corollary of the cause and effect law of karma, the doctrine of many lives, or reincarnation, is put into play. They are inseparable. For in a single life, it is quite impossible for all the ideal conditions to be present, so that each karmic effect from the past, as well as from one's current life, could be played out in the exact way, as to how it was ordained to be.

After all, the historical time has to be correct. And as well one's family members and the familial environment all have to be of the right choice; to create the ideal setting on the stage of life, so that the incarnating being can faultlessly enact the role he is destined to play.

In fact, this is just a small sample of the many complex choices that have to be so precisely coordinated.

Doesn't one ever wonder how come some children, at a very early age, exhibit a mastery over certain skills and abilities?

Take for example the five-year-old, who plays the piano like a maestro; or the four-year-old, who sings as though he's spent a lifetime at it. Or other youngsters being conversant and knowledgeable on subjects like geography, science, or astronomy at a level way beyond their limited years; the subject material so advanced that it is highly unlikely that they could have had access to it.

Well! Are these child prodigies created any differently from you and me? Or are they just exhibiting abilities that remain quite dormant in others though they possess them?

Surely most people who believe in a just and fair God being the Universal Father, know it's not the former.

So you might say, these kids just fall into a unique class. They are able to tap into their subconscious minds and awaken in their memories proficiencies and knowledge they once possessed, in a life before.

A phenomenon that doesn't happen that often. Although, the possibility certainly does exist, for each and everyone of us.

How many times in our lives, we are conscious that we are not knowledgeable about some particular subject. Yet, when someone starts speaking about it, we almost immediately and instinctively fall in line with the conversation, without a second thought, not realizing that it was there all along, somewhere in our subconscious. (Information we picked up some while back and had completely forgotten about.)

And that's because everything we hear, say, and do, is recorded in the subconscious mind, ready to be retrieved, under certain situations and circumstances.

This is not unlike what the child prodigies are capable of doing. Excepting that they are able to retrieve information and facts, from much further back in time. A super feat not too readily accomplished, by each and everyone.

Then again, there are quite a few documented cases of children making up seemingly highly fictitious stories of being in another place and time. Of having another family and describing in extreme detail what those relations looked like; the types of personalities they had; and what their vocations were, as well as their names, and so on. They are also able to describe vividly the grand occurrences that took place, not to mention giving the other names they were known by, as well as their occupations, at that time.

Interestingly enough, many of the facts from some of these cases have been verified. Either by researchers trying to bring some clarity to the doctrine of reincarnation by substantiating these claims. Or by "at-a-loss" parents, trying to put some sort of closure to the outlandish and incredible tales told by their "storytelling" children!

Here again, corroborating many of these ludicrous claims by kids who had had hardly any exposure to the outside world, can mean only one thing. There is more veracity to the doctrine of reincarnation, than one is made to readily believe in!

THE EARLY CHRISTIAN CHURCH

The early Christian Church, which was established in Rome, possessed many sacred, original, and priceless manuscripts.

But as time went on, beginning from the First General Council of Christendom at Nicaea in 325 A.D., to the Last Council in Constantinople in 869 A.D., many of these documents underwent major alterations.

Included in those changes in the "middle" of that period at the Second Council of Constantinople in 553 A.D., was the official removal of the writings on karma and reincarnation.

And for what might seem like a very good reason. As it was the belief, that if it weren't so, the church followers would see no pressing need for seeking immediate salvation. And hence, this would have no doubt weakened the authority, influence, and power of the church.

Ironically though, although these modifications were made, there are still some clear-cut cases of the doctrine of reincarnation in the Bible, (just as there are references to the law of karma). Which seems like more than a coincidence, wouldn't you say?

This is clearly expressed after Jesus had the vision of Moses and Elias on a mountain. The disciples asked him, "Why then say the Scribes that Elias must come first?"

And Jesus said, "Elias truly shall first come and restore all things. But I say unto you, that Elias is come already and they knew him not, but have done unto him whatsoever they listed."[29] Then the disciples understood what Jesus meant. He was referring to John the Baptist. Who then was obviously Elias, in his previous incarnation. Then again, when Jesus addressed the multitudes concerning John saying, "For all the prophets and the law prophesied until John. And if ye will receive it, this is Elias, which was for to come."[30] The reference here, is to John being the reincarnation of Elias, again.

SCIENCE NOT ALWAYS UTILIZED IN DETERMINING FACT

It is a well-known fact that verdicts in court cases are many times based upon the consensus of human testimony. And these decisions are made even easier, when the people who are in agreement are of a significant number.

We find in the social sciences, also, many facts and decisions are based on the gathering of information through extensive field work.

As is quite evident then, scientific proof doesn't always determine what is truth, or establish the basis, for what is fact!

In the same vein, more than just a few pieces of supportive information will be used, in trying to move the doctrine of reincarnation from the realm of belief to the realm of reality.

And in the hopes of trying to make the transition a lot more palatable, the credibility of the sources cited will be of the very highest caliber.

LORD KRISHNA SPEAKS ABOUT REINCARNATION

In the Hindu Bible, the Bhagavad Gita, from which a major part of the Eastern teachings on reincarnation is extracted, we find Lord Krishna enlightening his foremost disciple, Arjuna, by telling him: "Many, many

---

29   Matthew 17:10-13.
30   Matthew 11:13, 14.

births both you and I have passed. I can remember all of them, but you cannot."[31]

It somehow seems that there is something inherent in this statement as it tugs at one's subconscious, almost willing one to a trace of remembrance that you've lived before.

Lord Krishna further goes on to say, in the same chapter, "One who knows the transcendental nature of My appearance and activities does not, upon leaving the body, take his birth again in this material world, but attains My eternal abode."[32]

And giving us here, also, a hint at the workings of karma, he prophetically says, "The unsuccessful yogi after many, many years of enjoyment on the planets of the pious living entities, is born into a family of righteous people, or into a family of rich aristocracy."[33]

THE TWO BABAS

The millions of worldwide devotees of Sri Sathya Sai Baba accept him as the incarnation of the fakir, Shirdi Sai Baba[34], who departed the world in 1918 and who also performed many miracles.

Apart from him saying so, tales abound of Sathya Sai recounting to devotees, whom he knew when he was the fakir, details of their personal experiences with him in that lifetime.

Then again, there is the fact that he was born eight years after Shirdi's passing; the exact time Shirdi Sai Baba had said would elapse, before taking birth again.

A fascinating tale, which also substantiates this case of reincarnation, concerns the rani[35] of Chincholi, whose deceased husband—the raja, was an ardent devotee of the previous incarnation—Shirdi Sai Baba.

---

31   IV:5.
32   Bhagavad Gita IV:9.
33   Ibid VI:41.
34   A Moslem ascetic.
35   An Indian princess.

On learning that Shirdi Sai Baba had been reborn as Sri Sathya Sai and was residing in Puttaparthi, the rani paid him a visit and convinced him to return with her to the palace. A place he was no stranger to, as he'd often gone there, in his last incarnation.

As soon as he arrived, he startled the rani by immediately pointing out all the major changes that had taken place since his last visit. He indicated that there was no longer a margosa (neem) tree, that stood elegantly in the compound, and also that a well that was once there had since been filled up. Then he singled out a line of attractive buildings as being a new addition to the residential complex.

Most interesting though, was Baba's request to see a specific stone image that was in the palace; a gift to the raja when he had been in his Shirdi body.

This proved to be a slight problem, though, as the rani had never heard about the item before. After a thorough search, however, the item was soon located.

On this basis, along with several other intimate details that Baba seemed to know about her husband's life, the rani was quite easily able to accept him as no other than the reincarnation of Shirdi Sai Baba, whom her husband had so highly revered, when he was alive.[36]

SEVERAL CASES FROM A SPIRITUAL CLASSIC

Turning to the highly enlightening and uplifting classic, which has been in circulation for over seventy years, and translated into every major language. And which in 1999, was accorded the distinction of being included in the top one hundred spiritual books of the twentieth century by a Harper Collins panel of authors and scholars—*Autobiography of a Yogi*, contains several cases of reincarnation.

---

36 Excerpt from Howard Murphet's book: *Sai Baba Man of Miracles*, page 61. (Originally documented in Professor N. Kasturi's biography of Sri Sathya Sai Baba). New York, N.Y.: Noble Offset Printers, Inc., First American Edition, 1973.

And in this first episode there is also a supernal attestation, to this doctrine.

Paramahansa Yogananda, the author, in his incessant pleas to the Divine Mother;[37] to find consolation from the unbearable pain he felt, at the loss of his beloved mother, received this most reassuring and comforting reply: "It is I who have kept a watchful eye over you in each and every incarnation, in the form of your many mothers, there is no need to grieve, for I am truly, your only real mother."[38]

(Adamantine and ardent effort to commune with the Divine, transcends the insurmountable difficulties one normally encounters in trying to do the same, with a less prodigious effort).

As a youngster, Yogananda received an ancient amulet (which had mysteriously materialized between his mother's palms while she was meditating), from his brother, who was instructed to do so, by his mother on her deathbed, (within a specified time). He instantly recognized it as being from teachers of past lives, who were imperceptibly keeping a watchful eye over him, and guiding him on his path—to find God.[39]

THE REINCARNATION OF KASHI

In his ashram in India, Yogananda had a very affable and clever twelve-year-old disciple, named Kashi. On an outing one day, during a question and answer period, Kashi asked his master what the future held in store for him. To which Yogananda inadvertently replied, "You'll be dead soon!"

The disciple, taken aback, pleaded with his guru to promise that if his prediction came true that he would try to find him in his next birth, and guide him back onto the spiritual path again.

Kashi did pass away. And his guru, in constantly being intuitively vigilant for any signs of the vibrations of the soul of Kashi, in a new body, (as well as by utilizing secret yogic techniques), did indeed locate him

---

37   The personal aspect of God as Mother, embodying the Lord's love and compassionate qualities.
38   See chapter 2, page 18.
39   From page 23.

when he was reborn six months later, not far from a house he had resided in—when he was Kashi.[40]

THE AMAZING STORY OF MASTER MAHASHAYA

The story of the great spiritual master, Lahiri Mahashaya, (Yogananda's paramguru[41]), is one of the most fascinating to ever be recorded.

While casually wandering amidst the Himalayan solitudes one afternoon. He heard a very mysterious voice repeatedly calling his name, which he mistook for his mind playing tricks on him.

Tracing the sound to a cave, he encountered an ascetic, who surprisingly greeted him like an old friend who hadn't seen him in a very long time.

Nonetheless, Lahiri was quite taken aback when the ascetic asked him if he didn't recognize the neatly folded blanket lying on the ground, inside the cave.

Lahiri was just about leaving, thinking this to be one of the most bizarre experiences of his life, when the yogi then gently tapped him in the middle of the forehead, (the seat of the spiritual eye). Whereupon Lahiri immediately realized that this was Babaji, his great guru from his last life. And that the extra blanket, along with the water pot next to it, were his sole possessions from the latter part of his previous life. Which he had spent in deep meditation, next to his ever-watchful guru.[42]

SRI YOGANANDA THE ENGLISHMAN

In one of his many other books—*The Divine Romance*[43] Yogananda gives details of life from a specific incarnation.

On a visit to the Tower of London in the 1930s, he completely amazed the caretakers by revealing to them hidden chambers they didn't even

---

40   Recorded in chapter 28.
41   Guru of one's guru.
42   See pages 342-344.
43   Los Angeles, California: Self-Realization Fellowship, 2005.

know existed. Knowledge which he had from a previous life—when he was an Englishman.

Even as a kid he very much bewildered his parents by eating with a knife and fork—quite contrary to the Indian custom of eating with the fingers. A practice he instinctively knew he'd brought with him, from that same life.[44]

DÉJÀ VU

As if it were déjà vu, in another classic that continues to be a perennial favourite (reprinted over thirty times)—*The Third Eye* by Lobsang Rampa,[45] an author of eighteen other quite successful books, rich with knowledge on the deep science of metaphysics and the mystical arts, we find his guru Minyar Dondup telling him: "We have been close; and shared many experiences in past lives. This is clear to me; but of which, you cannot yet recall."[46] A statement that rings true, the almost exact words spoken by Lord Krishna, to Arjuna in the Gita.

"PREVIOUS INCARNATIONS"

One day, as part of his monastic training, Rampa was taken way below the main floor of a monastery, (into chambers he didn't even know existed). To observe the very unique process of mummification in gold, of an aged abbot, who had recently passed away. An ancient ritual reserved only for the highest lamas, who were also known as Previous Incarnations. (Attributed to the fact that they held a quite similar monastic status, in their previous lives.) After the completion of the laborious process, (which took several days), the body was transferred to another secret chamber, called the Hall of Incarnations. Where along the walls, could be seen lined up in majestic rows, a total of ninety-seven Previous

---

44 Excerpt from page 280.
45 Previously mentioned on page 7. New York, N.Y.: Ballantine Books, 1993 (twenty sixth printing). First published by Brandt and Brandt (New York), 1956.
46 Recounted on page 75.

Incarnations (going back to the earliest times); the golden mummified bodies, sitting in lifelike fashion, on golden thrones.

Being present here also, Rampa, for some strange reason, was mysteriously drawn to one particular figure, which seemed like an "old familiar friend," whom he'd once known.

At that point, as if reading his thoughts, Rampa's guide gently tapped him on his shoulder and said, "That was you, Rampa." Sending chills down his spine, as Rampa instantly recognized the mummified form as being "himself" six hundred years ago—when he was also an abbot.

Then his guide, filled with emotion, pointed out his own mummified body, which sat in ageless silence, next to Rampa's![47]

It is also a very intriguing fact to note that many Dalai Lamas were reborn to re-enact the roles they played in Previous Incarnations.

In Tibet, very young boys, at the tender age of three (an age when their minds are less likely to be influenced by outside factors), who exhibited unusual wisdom beyond their years and who recalled experiences from their last lives, were tested as Previous Incarnations. Being aware of their abilities, the parents would relay this information to an abbot, who would then promptly dispatch an investigating team to the child's home. Where they "put-together" a pre-life horoscope; and checked for telltale birth marks on the child's body.

If the boy is recognized by the monks, as to who he was "before," nine articles belonging to him from his previous birth, along with twenty-one similar items would be brought, from which he had to identify at least seven that were previously his. Only then, if he were successful, was he positively identified as a Previous Incarnation. (In the same way: the birth of a previous incarnation of a Dalai Lama was authenticated.)

From the age of seven on, the boy was resigned to spend the remaining days of his life in a monastery. Where he was intensely trained to fully awaken his dormant memories of the ancient wisdom he once had. As well as to learn the profession selected for him, by the most experienced

---

47   From *The Third Eye*, chapter 16.

astrologers, and to further enlighten him in the ways of the Tibetan spiritual teachings.[48]

Despite the more than adequate information provided to validate reincarnation, as a fact of "life" there still will be many skeptics.

Nevertheless, for the man who has found his unity with God. Reincarnation just happens to be nothing more than a byword, in his everyday vocabulary.

THE WHEEL OF LIFE AND DEATH

The wheel of life and death
Endlessly turning;
Like the cycle of day and night
Forever unswerving.

Will Father Time,
Without a care
Neutral like the cloudless sky;
Unlike mortal frames
That slowly age,
Then cease to be,
Put an end to this "dance macabre,"
Inherent, in each one—you and me?

The sweet answer—yes!
Like land and sea,
That will one day, no longer be
When Brahma's night[49] arrives eventually.
The rotating wheel

---

48   Recorded in *The Third Eye*, chapter 12.
49   Brahma's night and Brahma's day are infinitely long, fixed periods, when all creation dissolves back into Absolute Spirit, and emerges back into manifestation respectively, according to the ancient Hindu texts.

Of life and death
Comes to a halt also, incredibly.

Annihilation slowly reversing—
Once again resplendent,
With creation's dawn
(Also known as Brahma's day);
Night and day
Will soon return.

But the man of self-realization,
Who in times past,
Solved the mystery of his own creation.
No longer takes part
In God's new manifestation.
He was freed from nature's delusional cycles,
When he and his Heavenly Father
United as One!

CHAPTER 5 | The Wave and
The Ocean

Imagine yourself standing on the beach under a perfect blue sky, looking out beyond into the vastness of the ocean that stretches endlessly before you. There in your gaze you see only two things; numerous waves bopping up and down in an ever-continuous motion, settling down and levelling off, with their "mother"—the placid ocean.

At that point when a wave levels off. What do you see? You cannot differentiate between which is the wave, and which is the ocean! Is it not?

Probably the scene "tugs at your heartstrings" as unawares, the picturesque view subconsciously reminds one of a far deeper reality than that unfolding before you. (And that might very well be true.)

Many spiritually-enlightened teachers find this depiction of the wave and the ocean to be a very realistic analogy to man's own relationship of himself and his Creator.

The wave, in essence, having the same constituents as the ocean, and being an infinitesimal part of it can be likened to the soul of man, existing as a speck in the ocean of and being in each and every other way, indistinguishable from its greater self—Infinite Spirit.

The wave as is obvious too, is enveloped in an intransient "cloak" of froth. Which can also be compared to the soul of man, encased in a body of mortal flesh. A reference to which is made in the Bhagavad Gita; with Lord Krishna explaining to his devotee Arjuna, thus: "As a person puts on new garments, giving up old ones, the soul similarly accepts new material bodies, giving up the old and useless ones."[50] (And to show the universality of the existence of the soul, as taught by other scriptures.) There is also this declaration in 1 Cor. 3:16: "Know ye not that ye are the temple of God, and that the Spirit of God dwelleth in you." (The soul being synonymous, with the Spirit of God).

Coming back to the panoramic view from the shoreline. It is hard not to miss the effortless flow of the tiny wave over the majestic ocean. Firstly boldly rising up (as though to take a peek at its surroundings), momentarily sinking back, to rest upon the breast of its Source; only to continue on in its recurrent movement of endless oscillations. One may well wonder! Where this is all leading. But this cyclic pattern, mimics exactly the "journey" of the soul of man in its innumerable rounds of incarnations. Swimming for eternity, in the Ocean of Spirit with each crest of the wave representing a new birth and each dipping back into the ocean; man's departure from the shores of the phenomenal world.

But what happens if the wave ceases its undulations and permanently "flattens out" with the ocean? Then there is no way of telling one from another. Is it not? The wave becomes the ocean, and the ocean becomes the wave. One indistinguishable, homogenous unit.

In the same way, when man becomes self-realized and puts an end to his interminable incarnations, then his soul no longer exists as a separate entity but becomes one, with Changeless Spirit. A fact which is corroborated by Jesus in this statement: "Him that overcometh will go no more out."[51] (Meaning, he who attains self-realization, becoming one with God; will not take birth again).

And finally, a connection that should warm most hearts—the waves, in possessing inherent sameness, can be compared to the souls of "men,"

---

50   II:22.
51   Rev. 3:12.

which are identical sparks of divinity. A very profound truth corroborated by Lord Krishna thus: "I am the Supersoul seated in the hearts of all living entities. I am the beginning, the middle and the end of all beings."[52] In light of which: The Second Commandment as preached by Jesus to be one of the greatest: "Love thy neighbor as thyself,"[53] becomes all that easier to appreciate, when we realize—all men are truly brothers!

And on the other side of the coin, with man being a continuously incarnating being, Lord Buddha taught: Man should feel no animosity towards his fellow man, because, as a result of the countless lives he's lived; each person was part of another's family, some time or the other.

Despite, however, this great separateness that exists between soul and Spirit, there was a time when this "prodigal son" relationship was very much nonexistent. For all the major scriptural texts have made mention of the fact that God's first creations—Adam and Eve, were made in His very own image. As per this reference from the Bible: "So God created man in his own image, in the image of God created He him; male and female created He them."[54] Divine beings, who were empowered to use their divinely bestowed will to create their offspring by immaculate conception. (And not by the inferior method used by animals.) As the purpose of man's creation is to use his intelligence and ability to reason to acquire knowledge of the Spirit, which is latent within him. To which, he should make a consistent, and fervent effort, to realize. And to fall prey, to the sex temptation, a delusive counterpart to God's bliss;[55] is one of the most overwhelming distractions for him trying to regain—his divine status.

As a result of making the colossal mistake of doing what he was not supposed to do, with Eve "partaking" of the forbidden fruit in the midst of the garden,[56] Man fell from grace! and we became "victims" of the physical law of duality. Where birth must "unpleasantly" be followed,

---

52   Bhagavad Gita X:20.
53   Mark 12:31.
54   Genesis 1:27.
55   To be elaborated upon in chapter 13.
56   Genesis 3:2-3, 6.

by its opposite—death. And since then; man has unfortunately become estranged from his Creator![57]

In as much as we can all be reclaimed to our original status, as the "sons" of God; in the blink of an eye. By the mere fact, that man is endowed with free will—(given independence by God), to do as he pleases. The Creator will not thrust His will upon his children, for the Divine Father requires a sincere, from-the-heart effort, and use of free will when they are trying to reunite with Him, once again!

For if no compelling challenges are employed in the process, it is a regrettable fact, without a doubt, that man's fickle nature will surely predispose him to repeat his mistakes again. Where he once more falls from divinity, due to the absolutely compelling temptations of the material world. Even as Lord Jesus was tempted by Satan in the wilderness. And had to make a supreme effort in order not to give in to its tantalizing lures.[58]

As a result of him now being subjected to the laws of relativity, Man's once pure, controlled, "divine mind" has become subservient to the unruly senses. A prominent factor—which has made returning "home," more than a prodigious challenge.

As an example of how these five "wild horses" (the senses) hold sway, over the mind (the reins), of the human body (the chariot) in which the soul is a passenger: Imagine taking a walk in the park, on a bright sunny day. Where your attention may first be drawn, through the auditory nerve wires, to the wonderful sounds of the birds singing in the trees. Which in turn, may cause you to think about all the other wonderful sounds different species of birds might make. Then from your subconscious mind, a latent thought may arise, reminding you of a time when you were unceremoniously roused by a bird singing rather loudly, early one morning.

You may then enjoy observing the athleticism of a very fit jogger through your optical sense telephones. Which in turn, may trigger a

---

57   "Remember therefore from whence thou art fallen and repent" (Rev. 2:5).
58   Luke 4:1-8.

new thought of how some persons seem to make better runners than others. Whereupon another latent memory might arise, reminding you of a specific track meet—which took place, at the Olympics.

Then with it being a warm day, perceiving the heat through the tactual nerve centers, you may think of finding a nice, cozy spot, in the shade. Causing you to remember a time when you were able to be in the sun—all day!

Well! if this exercise seemed more real than imaginary. It's probably because one recognizes the pattern with which one's thoughts are constantly kept busy—each and every minute of one's waking state. (An endless parade of sensate impressions, followed by the arousal of new thoughts, which in turn cause latent memories from the subconscious to pop into the mind).

In this way, with the mind continuously preoccupied with some thought or the other, "travelling" inwards to realize one's true nature as an immortal, divine soul—has become almost an impossibility.

But, in much the same way as one can only discern the true and undistorted nature of the moon in a reflection of a body of water, when the surface is still, man can only realize what he truly is—when he is able, to still his own mind. "Be still and know that I am God."[59]

With regards to which, we even find reference in the Gita, with Lord Krishna telling Arjuna: "For him who has conquered the mind, the mind is the best of friends, but for one who has failed to do so, his mind will remain the greatest enemy."[60] Meaning: the uncontrolled mind (due to the senses), is our enemy, because it keeps us in delusion and vice-versa.

Here again, it is rather ironical too; how the external force of turbulence that prevents the wave from resting permanently on the bosom of the ocean isn't that much different from the turbulence of the mind—which plays a major part in preventing the soul from resting permanently in the bosom of Spirit.

---

59   Psalms 46:10.

60   VI:6.

Irrespective of his indifference to seeking out his true nature. It seems rather unjust that other distracting influences that move man in his current direction, away from his goal (and of which he doesn't have current knowledge), were set in motion, long before he put on the "outfit," of his current body; albeit, it is of his own doing.

KARMIC DEBTS

One of these already mentioned is the repayment of karmic debts, with which we entered the world. A compelling necessity in the purificatory process, before the soul, reunites with its Source. For make no mistake, (and there is no easy out); unless we become more selfless, compassionate, and loving beings—it could be a long time before this process can take place. As it is said, by seers of truth: We are constantly undergoing a minute shift in consciousness, in twelve-year cycles—moving us a little closer to the Creator. But unless this process is speeded up, those twelve-year cycles would add up to more years than we would care to imagine!

Nevertheless, naturally, like every exception to the rule, for those who make an effort to reach the Father, continually, earnestly, and with great devotion, virtually all barriers of separation, can be easily dissolved.

That there is no doubt, as far as this is concerned, the Bhagavad Gita, offers us this sublime assurance: "Even if one commits the most abominable action, if he is engaged in devotional service, he is to be considered saintly, because he is properly situated in his determination. He quickly becomes righteous and attains lasting peace."[61]

INHERENT TRAITS

Inherently too, we are programmed to behave according to the dictates of our karma. As we all "bring with us" three qualities (gunas), characterized in the Gita as the modes of goodness—(sattva); passion—having a great desire to work from morn to night (rajasa); and ignorance—subject

---

61   IX: 30,31 (verses also used in chapter three).

to the traits of anger, being quarrelsome, and having a very sensual nature etc. (tamasa).[62] And it is our karma, which plays a major role in determining in what proportions these traits are found within us!

Hence, it is quite easy to see why one possessing a preponderance of the less spiritual traits will find it a significant challenge to have a keen interest in spiritual matters or would care to find out why he was created in the first place. And only a rather dramatic event in one's life may actually bring about an overnight change, as one may have gathered, after reading chapter one.

UNFULFILLED DESIRES

Even more deluding than the effects of karma, is the mind's craving for sensual gratification, which creates an endless string of material desires. As a result of which, as long as they are unfulfilled, man must take birth again. For only in the material world can desires be fulfilled and only through the agency of the physical body—can they be satisfied. The grand reality being: Soul can only merge with Spirit when there is one desire—not for the gifts of the Creator, but for the Giver of gifts Himself!

As classic an example as can be found with regards to the delusory influence of desires, regards the great sage Lahiri Mahashaya, already mentioned in chapter four.

A great yogi, who spent the greater part of his former life in a cave, in intense meditation (almost at the point of union with the Creator). Yet, he was…forced to take birth again, all because of having a very strong desire to live in a palace. And if it weren't for his Divine guru—Babaji, materializing a palace to satisfy his desire, heaven knows, how many more lives would have had to be lived, before it would have been fulfilled.[63]

62　XIV: 5.10.
63　Excerpt from chapter 34 of Autobiography of a Yogi.

SELF-REALIZATION

One should not lose heart though, if the goal of life, the soul merging with Spirit seems to be an extremely formidable task. For the great sages do say: "Trying to attain self-realization, is like walking on a two-edged sword," (for temptation, like a shadow, is forever following us around). But when viewed logically, though, it does seem that is the way it is supposed to be.

For if fame, power, riches, and designations take such great effort, excess time, and endless commitment, to attain, doesn't it stand to reason that riches a sextillion times greater would require a much more substantial effort than that needed to attain material accomplishments? It would seem rather ludicrous, if one expected self-realization to be delivered on an "overnight platter!"

GAIN THE WORLD, AND LOSE THE SOUL

If we were to truly understand what Jesus meant when he said: "For what shall it profit a man if he shall gain the whole world and lose his soul?"[64] We should be able to conclude that to "gain the whole world" doesn't seem to be the ultimate goal of life. But rather has something to do with the soul. And that something is its reconnection with its Source.

In this context then, it's highly more logical why we should spend more time in pursuit of trying to realize who we truly are, and less in the accumulation of material things.

For as is so blatantly obvious, nary one black cent of our material possessions, which we worked so tirelessly to accumulate, would we be able to take with us when we leave the shores of this world. Nor will having riches in this life be any guarantee of what our status will be in the next.

While whatever knowledge we have acquired (stored in the bank of the subconscious) will always be a part of us. But it is only spiritual wisdom and experiences on the path of self-realization —that will easily resurface

---

64   Mark 8:36.

in our consciousness when we re-enter it.[65] So like the tributary flowing back into the ocean, we can continue our own journey into merging with the Ocean of Spirit. Hence, how easy it now becomes to see that there is hardly any comparison between the riches of the world and that, of the eternal soul!

THE PSEUDO SOUL

In essence, in much the same way as a piece of metal becomes rusted; subjected to the elements, such as air and water (moisture), our inner divinity—the soul, becomes "encrusted" with worldliness, and forgets its divine nature. Which results in man believing that the transitory part of his nature—the mortal body, with its personality and traits, to be his true identity. In so doing, his ego (body consciousness or pseudo soul), now acts like—the Doer!

THE CLASSROOM ANALOGY

It is wise to envision the earth as not being far different from a classroom. For just like a student who fails a grade is forced to repeat his exams before moving on to the next, Man must reincarnate again and again in the school of life, until he attains perfection, and "graduates."

GREAT PROMISE OF HOPE

There is a wonderful consolation, peace of mind, and a great promise of hope when one contemplates these timeless words from Lord Krishna: "Just fix your mind upon Me, the Supreme Personality of Godhead,[66]

---

65   "By virtue of the divine consciousness of his previous life, the yogi automatically becomes attracted to the yogic principles—even without seeking them... And when he engages himself with sincere endeavor in making further progress, being washed of all contaminations, then ultimately, achieving perfection after many, many births of practice, he attains the supreme goal" (Bhagavad Gita VI:44,45).

66   Same as anyone merged with Him. There being no difference in one attaining self-realization, and Him.

and engage all your intelligence in Me. Thus you will live in Me always, without a doubt."[67]

Now! Doesn't that sound like the wave; merging with the Ocean?

---

67 Bhagavad Gita XII:8.

THE WAVE AND THE OCEAN

Rolling over the tide of life
Never really feeling absolutely whole.
Isn't it strange?
Sometimes yes!
Even very alone?
My indiscriminate attachment to worldliness,
Makes me believe—
This is my home!

It seems rather odd, though!
Being at the top,
For only a short while
Then finding myself inexplicably,
In the bosom of the tide.

Where I feel, indescribable perennial peace
In the depths of my soul;
Unimaginably, like never before.
What a big surprise—
This is my true home!

Albeit only until I rise
To the crest, once more.
To continue one more lifetime
In my "delusional roll!"

CHAPTER 6 | The Divine Portals

 It is quite disconcerting to think that within each being resides divine centers of energy and light. Which, when we fully know how to "work" with them, allow us to realize that we are not the physical body, but are indeed spiritual entities. Yet, for many, there is no knowledge that such centers exist. And even for those who know how to "work" with them, there are some who don't fully understand what they truly represent.

Hence, it is easy to see how improbable it is to realize one's divine nature. When to pick the fruits of realization, one must first know how to climb the "tree" of divinity, and sadly for many, they aren't even aware that such a tree exists.

There are, however, more than a few examples of persons becoming aware of these centers, when undergoing heightened emotional experiences such as severe trauma, excess fear, intense sexual arousal, or who slip into a highly devotional state during prayer.

Unfortunately... it's hardly to their advantage, as they are unaware of how to harness this extremely dynamic energy to its fullest, or to capitalize on the experience as a stepping stone, for further spiritual growth.

These occult centers are what we know as the chakras, and the reason for calling them divine portals will become clearer as we move further on in the book. Chakra is a Sanskrit word meaning wheel, and rightly so, for the energy that radiates from them looks exactly like the spokes that radiate from the center of a wheel.

As for their locations, one may well wonder how come they are part of us, and yet, at the same time, so unfamiliar. And that's because the seven major chakras that are mainly written and spoken about, (and which are the focus of this chapter), are not within the realm of our everyday consciousness. For they are located in the astral body,[68] in the spine—called the sushumna; and the brain; which are counterparts of the same in the physical body.

The chakras, working together as well as individually, play a part in almost every conceivable aspect of the way we function as entities. That is, physically, mentally, emotionally, and that which is of most interest to us—spiritually.

As receivers, assimilators, and transmuters of life-giving energy, it is not too difficult to understand why these chakras possess such incredible and fascinating capabilities.

They're continually working for us, counteracting negative vibrations, in our continuous interactions with those around us. As well as battling the numerous types of inner "enemies" that invade us—such as bacteria and viruses.

But most importantly, it's their ability to link us to higher realities; bringing about inner awakenings to divine truths and enlightenment, which never ceases to amaze us.

Inherent within us, at the base of the spine, coiled up like a serpent in the lowest of the seven chakras, is our kundalini or evolutionary energy.

Although mostly dormant, there are always varying degrees of this divine current circulating throughout our systems, depending on our level of spiritual attainment.

---

68   A subtler body of light and cosmic energy, which enlivens its physical counterpart, and which is superimposed upon it.

Also within us, we have prana, or creative life force, (also known as cosmic energy), which is continually flowing and percolating throughout our bodies, and which is the essence that keeps us alive.

And when we are able to increase the flow of these two spiritual energies up the sushumna. (Which is why practitioners of advanced scientific techniques of meditation always keep the spine straight, so that these spiritual energies will have an unimpeded flow—up and down this "pathway.") Then the chakras—sleeping "lotuses" of light and energy, awaken. Their petals unfolding like flowers at dawn, reaching for the first sunlight.

When this occurs, we become more elevated in consciousness or spirituality, bringing about undreamed-of possibilities in our mental, psychical, and healing capacities. As well as bringing about changes in some who become less self-centered, and who now feel a lot more warmth and brotherliness toward their fellow humankind.

In essence then, apart from their many other functions, (especially the uppermost ones), the chakras control the degree and quality of our spiritual development.

The more "awakened" the petals, the higher the level and quality of our spiritual awareness; or you might say, the nearer we are getting, to mergence with the Divine!

As already mentioned, we all have subtle bodies—the astral, in which the sushumna is located. Within it exists another nervous system, which runs parallel to the one we're so familiar with. Consisting of an intricate network of nerve "channels" (called nadis) of a much more subtle nature dispersed throughout it. And incidentally, of which the sushumna is the main one. Where there is a preponderance of these nadis criss-crossing, that's where the major chakras are located. And conversely, where the intersecting is to a lesser extent—the minor chakras.

The latter are dispersed throughout this body, in such places as the back of the head, the palms of the hands, soles of the feet, in the chest area, and the temples, as well as at hundreds of minute points, all over the surface of the "skin," which provide the essence of the wonderful colours and energy patters seen dispersed, fluctuating, and vibrating throughout the aura,[69] that envelops the human body.

To the conservative minded (reading about the chakras and auras for the first time), this information will seem all a little too farfetched. Nonetheless, the following scientific data should help one to form a much more educated opinion.

Due in no small part to the tireless scientific research carried out by the Russian, Semyon Kirlian[70]—who invented Kirlian photography. We have for several decades been able to see what the aura looks like. Interestingly though, Kirlian photography shows that not only do humans have an aura around them, but every living thing that exists has one too. But even more fascinating is the fact that Kirlian photography shows if a portion of a leaf is "torn off," there is still a temporary aura remaining, matching exactly the piece that was removed.

And of interest, showing the profound influence of scientific spiritual practices on our being, Kirlian photography also shows the aura around someone soon after meditation as being many times more magnified and brighter than before the meditation began.

Returning more directly, to the topic at hand. Mention should be made of the outstanding work done by Dr. Robert Becker,[71] at the Veteran's Administration Hospital in Syracuse, New York. Dr. Becker was nominated in 1978 for the Nobel Prize, for his work showing that applying electrical stimulation could regenerate the missing part of a frog's leg. And that included nerves, cartilage, bone—the whole works.

From the results of his experiment, he concluded that for such healing, growth, and regeneration of a limb to take place, there must be focal

---

69   The aura's electromagnetic field extends from the human body in varying degrees from person to person. But a good gauge, for an average person, is between one to two feet.

70   Recorded in *The New Soviet Psychic Discoveries* by Henry Gris and William Dick. London, England: Sphere Books, 1979.

71   Documented in *Relief from Pain with Finger Massage* by Roger Dalet, translated by L. Zuch. London, England: Hutchinson, 1979.

points within the body that are able to magnify the electrical input of the energy originally applied.

Not only did he confirm his working hypothesis, but he found out that these focal points were known for centuries by the Chinese in their technique of acupuncture—used as a means of healing. As well as being found in the ancient writings of Eastern cultures like the Indians and Tibetans, in connection with the awakening of latent psychic abilities and their connections to altered states of consciousness. (And yes! These are no other than the mystical chakras—which this chapter is all about).

So, it is no wonder then that the seven major chakras, all have Sanskrit names. Although, in most books in the Western world, their much more simplified English "equivalents," are used.

Last but not least on the scientific front, another Russian, Dr. Viktor Adamenko went a little further with establishing the existence of the chakras, with the creation of a device known as the Acupointer; a miniature, battery-controlled pencil that lights up when it encounters a chakra, when passed along the skin!

But what is even more astonishing is the fact that the Acupointer is able to determine precisely the health of the person on whom the experiment is carried out. By the light on the indicator becoming dimmer when it encounters a chakra on the body of a subject who is sick.

Now that a presentation was made with regards to the overall picture of these occult centers of energy. The focus will now shift to the trees, and away from the forest.

MULADHARA (BASE)

The first major occult center is called the muladhara chakra, and it is located at the base of the spine, near the tailbone and plays a big part in the functioning of the adrenal glands, which produce adrenalin – that hormone which we are all so familiar with.

It comprises four petals, has a vibrant red hue, and to one in deep meditation – sounds very much like the humming "noise," made by that of the bumble bee.

This base chakra is responsible for our sense of survival. The way we react to danger—do we stay and "fight" or do we hit the road in a hurry? – A situation often referred to as the fight or flight syndrome, by psychoanalysts!

In this regard, with respect to our self-preservation, it governs all aspects of our everyday activities, such as our habits of eating and sleeping, our health choices, and even the depth of our spiritual convictions.

When this chakra is underperforming, we are incapable of standing up for our rights, being insecure and fearful, or even having an inferiority complex. So, it is not hard to see how this may result in a state of helplessness, causing one to become depressed, lacking self-worth, and experiencing feelings of vulnerability.

While on the other hand, an overactive base chakra creates an aggressive and dominant nature. Where one develops the attitude of having little regard for other's feelings, or what they may think. In a way, it engenders the disposition that only ruthlessness will get one to the top. Or, as you might say, only "the devil gets the hindmost!"

SVADHISTHANA (SACRAL)

The second center, called the svadhisthana chakra, is located two inches directly above the first and has six petals. Like the other chakras, it also governs a glandular "system" in the endocrine family; and in this case, it is the ovaries and the testicles. It has a bright, orange hue; like that of the sun, at sunset. And makes a musical sound, quite similar to that of a flute.

This spiritual center is oftentimes referred to as the emotional chakra; as it governs the way we express our emotions and how we respond to sensations of pleasure. So it should come as no surprise then, that it has a profound influence on one's "weakness for the other sex."

In this regard, when this chakra is overstimulated, it creates an insatiable lust for sensual gratification. And in an effort to make temporary pleasures more enduring, one may develop an addiction for sweet foods, and like a butterfly flitting from bud to bud, may find it hard to settle down and have a lasting relationship. Also this insatiable desire may lead to greed, as one tries vainly to fill the void, and lack of contentment, within.

On the other hand, if it is under-stimulated one may find it hard to truly enjoy pleasurable experiences – to let it all "hang loose," and have a good time.

And as a result, some may channel all of their energies into their careers; and along with that, becoming overly intellectual, — unnecessarily subjecting everything to intense analysis.

It is worth mentioning that getting back to nature and taking up simple hobbies like gardening, trekking, or outdoor sports, all act as a grounding mechanism, in maintaining balance in the second chakra.

MANIPURA (SOLAR PLEXUS)

The manipura chakra is the third psychic center, up in the sushumna, and it is located in the region of the solar plexus, just below and behind the navel.

As their functions become more complex and related to loftier aspects of divinity, we find that the chakras are composed of more petals, or rays of prana. And in this case, the manipura chakra is composed of ten. The colour of this chakra is a bright yellow; almost like a fully ripened, unblemished lemon – with a shine to it. And it governs the leydig gland, one of the least recognizable of the endocrine family, which is located just above the reproductive organ. A gland that has long been recognized to have a connection with spiritual and occult realities, by clairvoyants, seers, and mystics like Edgar Cayce,[72] and others.

---

72   Great American clairvoyant also known as the Sleeping Prophet (1877–1945).

Quite ironically, we are made to believe that heavenly music sounds much like harps playing, but, in fact, though, it most likely came about by the sound coming from this chakra heard by mystics and holy men, in divine contemplation.

The manipura chakra is the center of innovation and creativity. It controls our consciousness of will, influences our ability to make decisions, and has a strong hold on how we are able to shoulder responsibilities. Thereby playing a significant role in how confident we are, and it is not hard to find that one having this chakra well balanced – is well poised, achieves his goals, and possesses a very dynamic personality. In essence, it is the occult center from which mastery over material accomplishments can be attained.

When this chakra is fully awakened, it gives us our first exposure to the supernormal, and contact with the divine realms. Whereby we start to become aware of guidance from our divine selves – our souls, and also from our Spirit Guides,[73] who look over us as they try to advise, support and teach us, all the while allowing us to retain our free will. And not only this, but we become sensitive to the unseen, subtle, psychic energies emanating from – other people's auras.

When a person's third chakra is under-stimulated, he falls prey to being controlled by the ego, shutting out guidance from the higher realms and his Inner Pilot. It's a situation in which one finds oneself lacking motivation and confidence, being listless and slothful, and usually "wearing the cloak" of a yes man!

ANAHATA (HEART)

Next up on the "tree of life," is the anahata chakra, which has twelve petals and is located in the region of the heart. It has a beautiful, green colour like that of a tropical forest viewed from above. Its vibratory oscillations make the quite familiar sound, like the gong of a bell.

---

73   More evolved beings from higher dimensions.

And this chakra governs the functioning of a gland for which there is still some uncertainty as to what it actually does – the thymus.

There should be no surprise at the association which we're all so familiar with – between the physical heart and love. For it's the subtle heart center – the anahata chakra, which governs our capacity to feel love at all levels; love for ourselves, love for others, and for the essence of our being – the Divine.

In this respect, when this chakra is fully opened, we attain pure joy from within and become very happy being who we are. Which in turn, allows us to become more self-accepting, trusting, and less dependent on outward influences for our "fun and excitement." And at the same time, we are able to enjoy wonderful spiritual experiences, because of our newly awakened, expansive love for the Divine!

When we are able to feel love this way, it makes us very sensitive to the needs of others; we feel their pain and suffering and willingly reach out a helping hand to make a positive difference in their lives.

It is a noteworthy fact that some schools of meditation teach a technique that involves focusing on this chakra as a source of limitless, expanding love, which first envelops the body, and then continues on to encompass all things. And in so doing, awakens the quality of unconditional love (a divine quality). Thus allowing us the transformation to slowly become more and more like the true divine beings, we really are!

When the heart chakra is underdeveloped, we are still capable of giving love. But in this case, it is not quite so genuine. As it is usually out of obligation, or with an ulterior motive in mind.

Quite amazingly, those unexpected "hunches" we have felt at some time or the other, which surprise us with their accuracy, are actually subtle vibrations in the ether, which are picked up by the anahata chakra – which also acts as a very competent "receiving station."

There can be no disadvantages in having an overstimulated heart chakra, for in this case you might be much closer to fulfilling the purpose for which you were created than you might think!

VISHUDDHA (THROAT)

The sixteen-petaled vishuddha chakra, which governs the thyroid gland, is the fifth major occult center and is located at the base of the neck, just where it joins the spine. Its soothing blue colour, is very much like that we see in the sky on a bright summer's day. And its vibrational activities cause it to emanate a sound as of rushing waters.

This fifth chakra controls the consciousness of psychic or spiritual hearing; hence when it is opened, we are no longer just aware but can now clearly hear the thoughts of others (telepathy) and the voice of our eternal, divine self – the soul. And we are able to distinctly perceive the "words" coming through from our spirit guides, who are mostly unseen, although being – so very close to us.

Along with this marvelous gift, the vishuddha chakra also connects our consciousness to the subconscious mind – the storehouse of all impulses and experiences, and to the Akashic records.[74]

When this chakra is off balance or shut down, one connects to the lower or negative astral planes instead, and he begins to hear strange, disturbing inner voices that begin to confuse, depress, and coerce him. A situation which results in uncharacteristic negative self-dialogue, a lacking of initiative, and behaving in quite an unnatural way, in which the person is not even fully aware as to why, this is taking place.[75]

SAHASRARA (CROWN)

The seventh occult center; the thousand petaled lotus – "sits" atop the head and has great control over the pineal gland.

Just like the colours of the rainbow that range from red to violet (with each successive colour having a faster vibration[76] than the one before

---

74   A kind of central filing system with information of all events, thoughts, and actions, (past, present and future); located in the astral world.

75   The sixth chakra is given a full chapter —The Celestial Eye, which follows this.

76   It has now been established by both present-day scientists and ancient sages, that everything in the phenomenal world is formed by vibrations. So then, a colour could just as easily be identified, by the frequency of the wave it emits.

it), the colours of the chakras follow the same pattern, as each spiritual center vibrates faster than the one below it. Thus the crown chakra is violet in colour, but with a "tinge" of white in the center, as well. As might well be imagined, the sahasrara chakra, is the "grandfather" of all psychic abilities—it governs the consciousness of spiritual awakening and enlightenment. When it is fully opened, one can tap into the deepest mysteries of life and can get instantly the answers to the most perplexing questions of the universe. As the human consciousness is now one with the Universal Mind! The wave has become the Ocean!

A SCIENTIFIC ANALOGY

Scientifically speaking, it isn't that difficult at all to understand how the chakras are capable of becoming such powerful instruments for the awakening of psychic abilities. For just as a radio picks up electrical energy (radio waves) roaming in the ether, which one is not aware of, until the radio converts it to audio waves, in the same way, the chakras are able to modify the natural kundalini and pranic energies coursing through them, thereby altering the standard information we are programmed to normally receive.

In any event, is it any wonder, after realizing we possess all these extraordinary capabilities lying dormant in the chakras, we hear so often that – we only use ten percent of our human potential!

THE FIVE ELEMENTS

Included in the extremely remarkable teachings on metaphysical subjects—theoretical and practical, that our guru has imparted to us, his disciples, through his legacy of extensive writings (received from Self-Realization Fellowship).[77] There is reference to the five elements; earth, water, fire, air, and ether— (intelligent, structural forces responsible for

---

77   Which he established in 1920.

the manifestation of creation, including our physical bodies),[78] being "products," created by the first five chakras; each responsible, for the manifestation of one element. (In deep meditation, yogis[79] can perceive at the point of the "spiritual eye,"[80] these five elemental vibrations, as they pulse within these chakras).

But the deep, metaphysical significance of this fact, is that the three traits inherent in each being (sattva, rajasa and tamasa),[81] described in chapter five. Are actually inherent within each of these elements, in varying proportions. So it can easily be seen how the chakras are a phenomenal energy system. Apart from functioning at the level of spiritual awakening, they are responsible for the type of persons we are, and the very way we act too!

BIBLICAL SYMBOLOGY

Apart from the authentication of the existence of the chakras by scientific means, as well as by "mystical" practices. There is also a symbolic exposition of the chakras in the Bible. Which was taught to the disciples, by Lord Jesus.

For we find in Revelation,[82] that the great disciple John makes mention of the "mystery of the seven stars" and the "seven" churches. In fact, a direct symbolic connection, to the seven lotuses of light, described in yoga treatises as the seven "trap doors" in the cerebrospinal axis.

Obviously, not the conventionally accepted interpretation, but one, nonetheless, that makes further food for thought!

---

78   For example, without the earth element in creation, there would be no state of solid matter; or without the ether element, no background, to give expression to the phenomenal world.

79   Persons who use a scientific form of meditation to attain unity with the Divine – or realize his true nature, as being no different from his Creator.

80   The subject that makes up the content of the following chapter.

81   Only by the differentiation of pure, untainted Indivisible Spirit into these three qualities, could this world of duality come into existence—where everything is seen as a separation from a unity with the Divine.

82   1:20.

MOTHER EARTH

The "story" on the chakras would be quite incomplete, if one were not to mention (if only a few), that like the body, Mother Earth, "Herself," also has seven major chakras. All connected by an intensive network of connecting channels, called ley lines; just like the nadis, in the subtle body.

These are centers of high energy concentrations, where groups throughout history gathered to give thanks to Mother Earth for her supply of plenty, to invoke her blessings for future successful harvests, to go into mystic trances to foresee the future, and to seek spiritual inspiration through prayer, contemplation, and meditation.

The first chakra (base), is located at Mount Shasta, part of the Cascade Mountain Range in northern California. A place recognized as sacred, for centuries, by the Native Americans. And even now attracting New Age followers, who believe this energy vortex to be a source of mystical power.

Interestingly enough, in 1932, the occult sect – the Rosicrucians, popularized the belief that it was here the surviving people from the lost continent of Lemuria, made their new home.

Glastony Tor in Somerset, England, a place of power and potent transformational energies, as well as steeped in myth and legend from ancient times—is the location of the heart chakra (number four).

Apart from its association as the place where the Holy Grail is thought to be located, and where King Arthur and the Knights of the Round Table once held court. It's also quite ironic that it's here at the heart center, where one of the most fabled love stories of history took place; between King Arthur and his queen, Guinevere.

The crown chakra (number seven), is located in Mount Kailas, part of the Himalayan range, in Tibet – a region known as the "roof of the world." It should be no mere coincidence then, that the people of this land have always been attracted to matters of the spirit, with little regard for the accumulation of riches, or other transient things of the material world.

This sacred location is regarded to be the abode of the king of the yogis—Lord Shiva; from where his constant grace and divine energies pulse outward, to an unsuspecting world, just like our own crown chakra continually enlivens our lower chakras, by "feeding" them, with its spiritual energies.

SELF-WORTH

Irrespective of the degree of the lack of self-worth one may feel, it is consoling to always remember. The human body is a very sacred temple, a unique creation by the Heavenly Father. For only within the confines of the human body (the astral body is superimposed on it), can "centers" be found that have an untainted, direct link with the Creator!

THE DIVINE PORTALS

The divine portals,
Ever so near, ever so far:
Because of our unawareness,
Of their existence
Or where they are!

But once known,
Journey up this occult highway
To the Infinite
That leads us to the incredible realization,
Of who, we really are!

So do not procrastinate.
Find their locations,
And enter the other worldly portals,
That lead us,
To the supernal realms—
Where our mortality
Becomes a reality,
Of the long-forgotten past!

CHAPTER 7 | The Celestial Eye

 As an individual chakra, there has been probably more material written, more symbolic depictions, and more general discussions about this sixth psychic center, than all the others put together. In this respect, instead of the previous chapter being too long-winded and confusing, it was decided to allocate a separate chapter for the writings on the celestial eye, otherwise known in Sanskrit vernacular as the ajna chakra.

It is natural too, that for this reason, almost everyone has come across it – either directly or indirectly. Whether symbolically, in the movies, as the bulbous single eye in the middle of the forehead of ogres, and other mythical creatures. Maybe you've seen the mystifying words, "The Third Eye" on the cover of a book or were even curious enough to have perused such a volume. Or read about it in the holy texts, where it is referred to by such names as; the star of the East, eye of Shiva, the inner eye, dove descending from heaven, eye of intuition, and so on.

And even on an everyday basis it is not uncommon to encounter a dot of sandalwood paste in the middle of the foreheads of women from India, which is indicative of their traditional belief, whether consciously or unconsciously, in the existence of this sacred spot.

Falling into the third category, the second occult book to captivate my interest, "to investigate its contents," just happened to be – *The Third Eye* – a book which I already referred to in chapter one. Then years later,

I further elevated my understanding and knowledge of this enigmatic chakra, when I read *The Finding Of The Third Eye* by Vera Stanley Alder.

But nothing matches the much more profound and elaborate explanations and depiction of what the celestial eye is all about as when I learned about it through my guru's teachings and books.

As might be easily surmised, the celestial eye is located in the middle of the forehead, and just above the eyebrows in much the same position as it is depicted in the movies, and worn on the forehead by those in Eastern cultures.

(The big difference being, however, that it "operates" through an inner vision,[83] as opposed to how the physical eye functions.) Interestingly, we all unconsciously knit our brows, at this same exact spot, during a time of deep concentration. For this chakra just happens to be the seat of power of our will. And at the functional level, it signifies the unification of vision of the two physical eyes, as they penetrate into the higher realms where the veil of dualism falls away having "lost" its upholders of time and space.

One may look intently at this spot in the forehead, as do many practitioners of various meditational techniques, who focus their attention at this psychic center as part of their spiritual discipline.

But trying to see through the celestial eye can prove to be quite challenging. For not only does it involve deep concentration and extreme calmness, but more importantly, one needs to be instructed and guided by a bona fide spiritual teacher, who himself has accomplished the feat of opening this psychic center. And as such, can competently guide his disciples to do the same.

---

83   Nonetheless, highly advanced yogis, and devotees steeped in a life of intense prayer, who have reached self-realization; can see through this "eye" whether with the physical eyes opened or closed. A blissful superconscious state referred to as: nirbikalpa samadhi.

DESCRIPTION OF THE CELESTIAL EYE

Most of us can see an astral light,[84] after focusing on this spot for some time, which is quite discernible as being a mellower version than that we are accustomed to. And after our concentration deepens, a dark spot referred to as the bhramari guha in the yogic texts usually begins to appear in the center. In as much as the word bhramari guha has three distinct and appropriate meanings, the one selected to be used here will be: revolving. For as the meditator who knows how to open the celestial eye steadfastly perseveres, the two powerful forces; avarana (a veil-like power), and vikshepa (a scattering power) that prevent "entry" into the bhramari guha, begin to decrease their protective influence. As a result, the dark spot slowly begins to rotate, revealing a sphere of golden light, (which is more of an aura than a distinct colour) within which one sees another sphere of brilliant blue (the most pronounced hue of this chakra). And in the center of this, the meditator beholds the goal of his tireless efforts; a white, palpitating pentagonal star,[85] betokening that the celestial eye is now fully opened.

It is interesting to note that each of these sections is a microcosmical representation of aspects of the Creator in the macrocosm. Although these divine aspects will be explained further in another chapter. It can be said here, that the golden halo represents the divine, omnipresent vibration—Aum, which structures and upholds all creation, also known in the Bible as the Holy Ghost and appropriately so, for like a ghost, it does seem chimerical, not readily perceptible to the senses.

The indigo-blue sphere represents the universal intelligence of God in all creation (Christ Consciousness) as it exists within this vibration. Or

---

84 Although most of us will find it difficult to penetrate further into this tunnel of omniscience. To sit for a few minutes daily (ten minutes to start), focusing at this spot, although not bringing about great realizations; will prove quite helpful in calming the storm of the restless mind. Sitting with spine upright and breathing calmly and slowly for a few minutes before commencement should be incorporated into the technique. As well as, sitting calmly for a few minutes after completion. For many, mastering this technique will create a longing to seek out more advanced forms of meditation.

85 Excerpt from *Autobiography of a Yogi*, page 311.

one might say, a reflection of the Uncreated in the created, referred to as God the Son and Tat, in the Christian and Hindu scriptures respectively.

As might be expected, almost everyone should be quite familiar with this concept; for all the major scriptures proclaim that the Divine is manifest in everything and everywhere. And this is why, Jesus is called the Son of God, because this Christ Consciousness that lies latent within all of us was fully manifest within him – there being no difference between him and the Father. They are one! The wave had become the Ocean.[86]

And finally, the pentagonal star is a representation of the Divine, as He "exists" beyond His vibratory creation, in his transcendental realm as Absolute, Uncreated Spirit! As "head of the hierarchical system of creation," He is appropriately referred to as: God the Father, or Sat.[87]

COMPARISON TO THE PHYSICAL EYES

While still on the topic of associations, if one may not have discerned by now, the physical eye and the celestial eye do share a few similarities.

The golden halo, which comprises the largest part of the celestial eye, corresponds to the white section of the physical eye, which constitutes the largest part of the same. The brilliant blue sphere to the pigmented part of the physical eye – the iris. And the pentagonal star, which signals the opening of the celestial eye, to the pupil, which lets light in and similarly creates the function of vision.

(And here is as good a spot as any to mention—Apart from having its feature colour like the other chakras, this one also controls a gland – the pituitary).

---

86   "Believe me that I am in the Father, and the Father in me" (John 14:11).

87   In Sanskrit vernacular: Absolute Spirit.

RANGE OF VISION

Vision through physical eyes gives exposure to the phenomenal world, manifested and existing because of the Divine's intelligent vibrations, which structure and hold every part of creation together. Keeping the soul attached to body consciousness and its ceaseless demands for fulfillment of its endless desires, and being true to its false nature – the ego, trying to lord it over the material world.

However, when the celestial eye is opened, an entirely new perspective dawns upon the fortunate few. For they not only behold the scenes of the entire physical world. But through their "new-found" supernatural vision, they see into the hidden subtle realms of the heavenly kingdom, where everything far outshines in beauty anything we can see or even begin to imagine in the physical world.

With vision that "operates" in every direction simultaneously, they can observe what is taking place anywhere in creation and effortlessly project their consciousness there. The veil is lifted from the phenomenal world of duality, and the mysteries and realities of all the different realms are no longer a secret but become like an open book before their spiritual gaze. And if they so desireth, the past history and future destiny of anyone and any place can also be instantly revealed.

The opened celestial eye makes one able to see the divine entities carrying out their official duties as part of the spiritual hierarchy, (including our Spirit Guides), although now, we may not really need their assistance.

While within our own earth realm, one can witness the ever-present magical interplay of fluctuating colours around human bodies –the aura, and behold the source of their otherworldly energies – the chakras.

With the consciousness encompassing omnipresence, the one with the ajna chakra opened hears the divine sound Aum, emanating from every particle of creation – an almost exact replica of the mighty roar of the ocean. A culmination of all the other enchanting sounds heard when the other five lower chakras are opened.

ALL CREATION VIBRATES

In the normal frame of reality, the concept of the celestial eye and its incredible functions all seem a little too farfetched. But to show that they are all within the realm of logic, it is necessary to look at what comprises the essence of every particle of creation – which includes both the intangible and the concrete. And that essence happens to be energy; everything that exists is comprised of energy. A fact which has been scientifically proven to be absolutely factual, and also confirmed by those who have attained the state of God-realization. As a corollary to this, it means everything at the minutest level is not inert but is always vibrating (the divine Aum vibration), or put another way – is constantly emitting vibrations!

Interestingly enough, Dr. Hippolyte Baraduc, a renowned French physician and parapsychologist of his time, over a century ago, actually invented a machine that shows that thoughts emit vibrations. And although digressing for a second, he also snapped a picture of his wife's astral body, disengaging from the physical, at the time of her passing. (But like everything of this nature, it's what you see in it!)

AN AMAZING "ORGAN"

As we know, our optical nerves pick up vibrations of a limited range, which are relayed to the brain and analyzed by the "operator" – the intellect, enabling us to see an endless stream of things on the physical plane. However, there are super-rapid vibrations that come after the colour violet on the scale of vibrations, which are quite impossible for us to "pick up"; for example, x-rays, which vibrate at two trillion vibrations per second. Or those categorized as electric and magnetic, which oscillate so quickly that their frequencies haven't yet even been realistically defined. That penetrate so easily through solid matter that they simply pass through the lens of the eye without us being aware of their presence, but the reality being – this does not mean that they do not exist.

But if we ask the question; "Is there an organ we possess that can be utilized to detect these super-rapid vibrations that pass through matter like a knife through butter?" The answer is yes! (as we've just discussed), the celestial eye – but only when it is opened. But the concept becomes all that much more credible, if we were to appreciate the fact that it is not located in the physical body but in the much more highly developed, more spiritually attuned astral body. That, for all intents and purposes, is the constant "life-giver" to the physical one.

MAN'S BEST FRIEND

It's a very strange thing, but growing up in the old country, we were often told by the elders that the eerie sound of a dog's howling, (a sound that is completely different from the characteristic bark of a dog, and usually occurring at night), was a sure sign that someone close was soon to die. And as amazing as it may sound, they were correct – most of the time. A situation that may appear purely coincidental but can be explained by a dog having a super-keen sense of vision, not unlike when the celestial eye is opened!

For in such instances, it sees the astral form of a family member or an acquaintance returning from the astral world, to guide the "departing one" on their journey to the other side. Or, the astral form of the dying person, outside of the physical body preparing for the journey "home." (But with the ties to the silver cord,[88] not completely severed). And as such, it is simply a case of the dog expressing its grief at losing a friend. For in most cases, the animal had a close connection with the one soon to be deceased.

It is a known fact that dogs and other animals can "pick up" vibrations that we can't. For there are also recorded cases of ferocious dogs – trained to kill, yet acting quite the opposite when they sensed their intended victims did not exhibit any fear, which turns out to be a case of them "picking up" another one of those vibrations that escapes the human capability.

---

88   An infinitely long, intangible cord that connects the physical to the astral body in much the same way the umbilical cord connects a baby to its mother. When it is severed, what we know as human life, has ended! – a very brief reference is made of it in the Bible (Ecc. 12:6).

And finally, there is that unique dog whistle, which is completely inaudible to human hearing, but is easily heard by a dog. Showing again another sense in a dog being much more highly developed than it is in us humans.

WISDOM OF THE ANCIENTS

Many ancient cultures had full knowledge of the celestial eye. For long ago, man lived more in tune with nature and God. Plus they partook of purer and simpler foods, which did not block their chakras.

We know life was pristine, the air was fresher, and there was less attraction to the things that now keep our senses totally focused outward, enabling people to be much more receptive, (with training) to the opening of the celestial eye.

For example, the Egyptian and certain Eastern cultures displayed upon statues of those renowned for their wisdom, a knob, or some other feature in the middle of their foreheads.

There were sacred ceremonies and rituals routinely performed in the Egyptian temples, where virgins led disciplined lives, trained vigorously, and prepared for the opening of the third eye on their way to becoming clairvoyant and possessing other psychic powers. As a matter of fact, the ancient libraries of Alexandria; onetime esteemed capital of Egypt, (and one of the main centers of knowledge in the world), were known to house the not-so-easy-to-find volumes on this, one of the most esoteric subjects, of the ancient wisdom.

In Tibet, the land that time has forgotten, home of an abundance of monasteries, and steeped in the tradition of mysticism and spirituality, uniquely gifted boys, from a very tender age, were led by their gurus through a definite spiritual "system," to the opening of this all-seeing eye. It is with this vision that the Lord Buddha was able to review all the countless lives he once lived. (That is why it is not unusual to find most statues of the "Enlightened One," with a dot in the middle of the forehead.)

But, faster living, rapid progress in the age of materialism, a lack of conviction to observe the perquisites like self-control, and undergoing life's ups and downs with more of a less agitated mind. Along with the fact, that when psychic power is used for selfish means, material gain, and to cause harm to our fellow man. All these things contribute to making the opening of the celestial eye that much more of an onerous task. And as the years rolled on, the connection with this spiritual center just fell into the realm of the apocryphal.

Nevertheless, there is still a meaningful number of people in the world, (although not basking in the spotlight of the public eye), who still possess the function of the ajna chakra. As well as a tiered platform of persistent practitioners, who are all on their way to eventually succeeding at accomplishing this esoteric feat.

BIBLICAL REFERENCES

Addressing the holy scriptures, it is an extremely amazing fact, that this seat of spiritual vision is alluded to in the Bible. For we find it says; "The light of the body is the eye, therefore when thine eye is single, thy whole body is also full of light, (for when the celestial eye is opened, one sees clearly within himself, the same creative energy that is instrumental in producing all of creation), but when thine eye is evil, thy body is also full of darkness. Take heed therefore that the light which is in thee be not darkness."[89]

Then again, we find a repeat of the same proclamation, in another part of the volume; "If therefore thine eye be single, thy whole body shall be full of light.[90]

And although this next quotation is steeped in symbolism, if we attentively study the references, it will paint a much clearer picture than what first "meets the eye." "Afterward he brought me to the garden, even

---

89   Luke 11:34, 35.
90   Matt. 6:22.

the gate that looketh toward the East . . . and his voice was like a noise of many waters, and the earth shined with his glory."[91]

As we all know, a gate is a structure built about an entrance, which is capable of being opened or closed. Similarly, the two protective forces vikshepa and avarana can symbolically be viewed as a gate, for they have the ability to open or close entry into the "tunnel" of the celestial eye. The direction of the east, as we are too well aware of, is the direction from which our planetary sun rises. Likewise in this quotation, the East can be alluded to the "sun" of the heavenly eye, in the middle of the forehead.

Next, the noise of many waters, as we have already mentioned, is the sound heard by the ever-persistent devotee when this sixth chakra is fully opened.

And finally; "The earth shined with his glory," can be referenced to the unique and totally majestic view that can only be perceived through this psychic center.

As we know, it's not unusual to find different interpretations to what is written in this holy book. Nevertheless, the interpretations here should do no more than provide poignant food for deeper thought!

THE FINAL EXIT

It is surely ironic that while in the body, we are not even aware of this spiritual center, yet at the time of departing it, it's to this holy spot that man's consciousness is involuntarily drawn. For man's astral body makes its final exit through the "tunnel" of the spiritual eye, which accounts for the upraised eyes found in those on their journey to the other side.

And this is why we hear the extraordinary stories from the very fortunate few who have returned to life, (after been pronounced clinically dead), describing their exit out of the body, as journeying through a tunnel of brilliant, white light. Which fits the description exactly of what

---

91   Ezekiel 43:1, 2.

one sees, when his focused gaze penetrates the pentagonal star, of the celestial eye.

As is clear from this chapter, the opening of the chakra in the middle of the forehead reveals the mysteries of creation in a way few other practices do. So when this can be accomplished, then there will be no doubts as to the answer of the "most" perplexing question; "Man to God"—is it truth? Or is it fiction?

THE DIVINE EYE

The divine eye,
Unlike the physical eye,
Is not in the physical body.
The divine eye,
Unlike the physical eye,
Does not see unreality.
The divine eye,
Unlike the physical eye,
Does not have limited vision,
But for all intents and purposes
Can be said to be all-seeing:
Seeing into every nook and cranny,
Perceiving every realm of God' creation,
This inner astral vision reveals
The past, present, and future.
But most importantly,
Seeing our own reality—
Our inherent, latent divine nature,
Is the greatest realization!

CHAPTER 8

It's a Starry, Starry Life

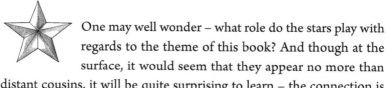 One may well wonder – what role do the stars play with regards to the theme of this book? And though at the surface, it would seem that they appear no more than distant cousins, it will be quite surprising to learn – the connection is more like a parent, and an offspring!

To more than a few, it is common knowledge that the configuration of the stars in the firmament on the day and precise time of birth, as well as the exact location of one's conception, give a map of events that have a very high probability of taking place in one's lifetime. Along with a more than fairly accurate indication of the traits we bring into the world, our strengths and weaknesses, and the unique way each and every one of us, reacts to our worldly experiences. But beyond this, a clear understanding of the mystical, intricate, and otherworldly connection between man and the planetary bodies, is somewhat obscured. As this relationship is hardly ever touched upon or fully elucidated in writings on this precise, complicated, and in-depth science – oft-times referred to by mystics and self-realized masters—as the "Song of the Stars"—and known to us as astrology!

It is said that the rays emitted by the celestial bodies at the time of birth send forth those positive and negative vibrations that fashion the exact characteristic makeup we have, preplanned in the astral world, to work with in this lifetime – to learn the lessons we are now prepared to experience – in our evolution towards mergence with the Divine!

CERTAIN CULTURES

A little background on the great importance the science has had in certain cultures, up until the not-too-distant past, will indicate just how dependent people were on the "heavens" for guidance in their everyday lives! And should contribute to acknowledgement of the authenticity of the art!

It is no secret that it was in such lands as India and Tibet that the science of astrology was held in the highest esteem. (And for good reason too, for it was only in those lands that the most highly skilled astrologers could be found.) It was very much a common practice within the homes of the wealthy, (including those of royal birth), to have a horoscope cast for their children, even while they were still young. And probably because they were the only ones who could afford it!

SOME SPECIFIC READINGS

Being of noble birth when he came into the world, several decades ago, the Tibetan holy man, Lobsang Rampa, was no exception to the rule. He had his horoscope cast at the tender age of seven and became aware that he was destined to become a doctor and a skilled astrologer and would journey to the West, where his teachings on the fascinating "world of the occult"–both theoretical and practical, would not be well received. (And like everything else that involves man's consciousness when it is capable of comprehending the "unknown"—those things become part of the mainstream, as did his writings on those subjects, many years after they were "released.")

Then, ironically too, it was because of what the horoscope "pointed out" for the young prince, Siddhartha Gautama, that his father was so adamant that his son should not leave the confines of the palace grounds.

As it foretold He was very highly destined to give up all worldly possessions – become a renunciant—and go in search of truth!

Another great personage to have his horoscope cast, was Yogi Paramahansa Yogananda. Part of which can be viewed to be somewhat humorous, rather than being entirely factual. For it pointed out that he
would be betrothed three times. But in as much as the prediction was
along the right lines, (as he was matched up three times), the sacred
vows never took place, for the holy one had his mind set on a union of
a much higher order!

The silver lining here is that fate is a poor "controller" of one possessed
of an indomitable will. For deep within us, we have resources, (though
not readily accessible), that can rewrite any script that we are destined
to follow. And so it was with the great yogi; his uncompromising resolve
was so strong to find God that fate became a poor director of his destiny.
(Incidentally, the famed Greek philosopher, Socrates, used the strength
of his will too, along with intense self-analysis, to change the course of
his life, for he felt very strongly he possessed the ideal traits to become
a murderer.)

Returning to astrological charts, it should be pointed out that there are
so many variables and permutations of factors to take into consideration
when doing an astrological analysis. That sometimes, a very inconspicu-
ous bit of relevant data escapes the eye of even the most expert astrologers. (Not unlike other professionals like surgeons, engineers, and pilots,
who have all been known to have erred.) As there would have been some
indication on the yogi's astrological chart as to the chances of the three
weddings not taking place.

In the book *Nityananda The Divine Presence*, there is a good example
of how such miscalculations are very likely to take place. It was not uncommon for the master, not only to guide his devotees on the spiritual
path, but to give them direction on how to become happy and successful in their worldly lives as well. Assisting a close devotee who was very
desirous of getting himself a "life-companion," the master pointed him

out to a family in his presence who were also seeking someone for their eligible daughter.

Immediately after the match was arranged, the horoscopes of the couple were dispatched to several professional astrologers, to see if their astrological charts were compatible. In every single case, the astrologers were in agreement that the marriage would not be an appropriate one. Nevertheless, when Nityananda was notified (although he did not see the horoscopes), he quickly pointed out an aspect in the charts that nullified the facts upon which the astrologers had based their decision. A point that had completely bypassed the scrutiny of the several expert astrologers, who were now in total concurrence with what the master had to say.

Coincidentally, even the author of this volume on the master falls into the category of having his horoscope read, (although not characteristically at an early age). One that amazingly told of his meeting with a great being at age twenty-eight, whose name starts with the letter N. And also which accurately gave a few not-so-well-known details about the great being's life.

Not only were personal horoscopes a common feature in these cultures, but major events in everyday life were also planned according to the alignment of the bodies in the heavens.

The holy men, skilled in the art of astrology and well aware of what the configuration of the celestial bodies "bring about" on a daily basis, made sure to plan their "many-day" religious ceremonies when the earth was in a strategically auspicious configuration with regards to the sun and moon. As this special arrangement is more accommodating to the human mind being in a less turbulent state, and more conducive to prayer, contemplation, and meditation.

THE SPIRITUAL CONNECTION

Now that an introduction to the art of astrology has been completed, we'll look at the mechanics of how the configuration of the inanimate bodies in the heavens exert their extraordinary influence upon our own everyday lives!

As already mentioned, "within us," we all have the three qualities of goodness, passion, and ignorance, which are inherent in the five elements – found in the lower five chakras. But as incredible as it may sound, it is the rays emitted from that specific alignment of heavenly bodies at the time of birth that mete out the precise proportion of these universal traits. And along with this exceptional phenomenon, it also serves as the "blueprint" that objectifies the karma that we each have brought with us as we "journey on" in the current incarnation.

Also within man, there is a microcosmical astral system with six inner constellations, (twelve by polarity); rotating around the sun of the all-seeing celestial eye. This system, in fact, corresponds to the twelve astral signs of the zodiac. And hence it is interrelated to the macrocosmical system of the physical sun, and the twelve zodiacal signs. Which should make it a lot easier to understand why the programmed information (resulting from the alignment in the heavens), manifests through the "factory" of these divine centers – the chakras.

And it's because of this pronounced interrelationship too, between the chakras and the twelve signs of the zodiac, that man's consciousness expands ever so slowly, (in twelve-year cycles), on its journey to union with its Creator!

The connection of the body of man with the "solar system" doesn't end there, for even a day is segmented into four periods that have a vibratory relation with the rotating seasons of the year, which essentially effect microscopic changes within our bodies. (And this is why it is not uncommon to experience states of fluctuating temperaments within a twenty-four-hour period.)

The hours from midnight to six in the morning correspond to spring; from six to midday — summer; then from midday to six in the evening correlates to autumn; and the final six hours of the day have a connection, with winter.

This understanding of these distinct four periods of the day are put to good use by practicing meditators, as they have learned from their enlightened gurus to meditate at certain hours within those four periods, so that they can have better control of their minds.

And finally, even the physiology of our bodies, (and hence our health), may not be able to escape from what is "written in the stars." As biochemists have postulated that the twelve main salts found in the human body like; potassium phosphate, sodium chloride, and iron phosphate, etc., (to name a few), are all governed by the twelve signs of the zodiac.

And the one generally utilized the most in our bodies, is the one associated with the astrological sign under which we were born. As we are prone to perform activities that entail using up more of this salt over the others. A situation that results in the ills that trouble us, being a direct consequence of having a shortage of that diminished compound.

For example, an Aquarian whose "birth" salt is sodium chloride, having a shortage of this compound may end up suffering from jaundice and conditions of weakness in the body. As this salt is responsible for the distribution of water throughout their systems.

What this all means then — this intricate association of man, astrology, and divine knowledge, is that despite one's most highly honourable intentions to think spiritual thoughts or to have a genuine desire to inquire about the mysteries of life, Man will, more often than not, be irresistibly and constantly drawn back to move along the path that has been laid before him "by the stars," even if it keeps him in delusion — indifferent to matters of the spirit!

At this point, it would be fair to say the astrological "picture" would seem somewhat incomplete if a "few words" were not said about the general behaviours we "inherit" from the "cosmic forces" when we take birth, under a specific zodiacal sign.

ARIES

(March 21–April 19)

Aries is the first sign of the zodiacal year, which commences on March 21st, at the time of the vernal equinox. Like spring, which is a time of rejuvenation and new beginnings, Arians bubble with creative energy, and along with their impulsive nature are initiators of action in the development of new projects. Although, it's because of their impulsiveness and unrelenting drive that they proceed headlong into projects without having their plans fully worked out or sometimes lacking the expertise or experience for the job at hand. It's not of great consequence though, as by their very nature – they are risk takers – by birth!

Also, it's because of their rash temperaments, along with their lack of wherewithal to analyze who they are dealing with, that Arians can quite easily be deceived.

Tending to be fiercely independent because of their superior minds and being born leaders, Arians do not fit the part – of playing second fiddle!

Because they are always using their minds, (and not adventitiously so), for this sign rules the head, Arians will find it very beneficial to take time to relax their overworked minds and to make sure they always get plenty of rest, as they usually suffer from headaches, and migraines as a result of putting too much stress, in the "head area!"

TAURUS

(April 20–May 20)

Following Aries is the sign whose symbol is the bull—Taurus! And like the bull, whose disposition exhibits obstinacy, we find this trait quite common among Taureans. Added to this connection, we find that in the same way as a bull market represents growth in investments (stock prices going up), people born under this sign may be said to have a special knack of healthily" growing their own wealth.

Folks "taking birth" under this sign, although not excessively ostentatious, do like to surround themselves with things of beauty, not to mention having an irresistible weakness for elegant clothing.

They are not overly motivated and don't aggressively pursue their goals like people born under other signs. Although, when they attempt "a go" at them, they usually accomplish what they set out to do through tenacity and intense perseverance!

Although it may be said Taureans do not wear their emotions on their sleeves, they are quite trustworthy, and they can be counted on for their reliability. And if you really take the time to know them, the cloaks they wear are shed and they appear just as sociable as those who are good at being so.

Taurean folk have a deep appreciation for Mother Nature, and if they so desireth, can become quite proficient in vocations connected to the "land."

Because of their indulgence in excesses of the "taste buds," they tend to become susceptible to ailments stemming from being unable to keep their appetites in check. Added to this, because of their nature to not openly express their emotions as well as not to freely give expression to their creative energies, we may find this attributing to a connection with thyroidal problems!

GEMINI

(May 21–June 20)

Persons born under Gemini, the third sign, are usually quite perceptive, as they tend to have the ability to see into both sides of a situation. (A "gift" of being born under the sign that has the twin brothers – Pollux and Castor as its symbol.) As they represent a mind with a twofold nature! Because of this too, Geminis are usually quite capable of maintaining balance in their lives —not overextending themselves in their careers – taking time out when necessary, "to bask in the sunshine." This is an important factor in their lives, for as long as they don't overwork their nervous systems, they can retain a very sharp intellect. The converse is true too, as losing the edge in this balance, by putting extreme pressure on their minds, can result in breathing problems and more serious respiratory conditions.

Being born under this sign "translates" into one inherently "bringing" a wealth of worldly experience, which in turn results in Geminis being "Jacks of all trades," and like a chameleon, they are quite adaptable to most of life's situations. Consequently, in spreading themselves too thin, they usually find it somewhat difficult in achieving the level of expertise in some fields that they are keen in pursuing.

Sharing and communicating new ideas and information, on whatever fascinating facts they may "run into," as well as learning new things, play a big part in the life of a Geminian. And if they think they are not doing enough in this area, then they may even turn this passion into writing as well!

Interestingly enough, in some Geminis the influence of the twins (depicted in Greek mythology as one human, and one divine), might be so overwhelming that occasionally, one may actually believe they are seeing "two people in one!"

CANCER

(June 21–July 22)

Cancer is the fourth sign of the zodiac. One that is ruled by the moon. Which makes people born under this sign less reliant on reason and more vulnerable to the influences of the emotions. They are openly loving, nurturing, and endearing characters, who thrive on social interaction. Hence, they are fond of entertaining and initiating social gatherings and are good at forming strong family ties – earnestly believing in the sanctity of home life.

"Cancer-borns" are strong willed, laborious, and tenacious, and can accomplish whatever it is, they set their minds to! Curiously enough, though, like the crab (the symbol of cancer), that effortlessly motions forward as well as backwards. It's not unusual for them, after investing passion, energy, and time into a project, to unexpectedly hit the reverse gear and leave things unfinished.

At times boredom sets in, their adventurous spirit urges them to take in a change of scenery, and they take off on impromptu travels!

Although not quite noticeable, their feelings are easily hurt. A situation they need to work on to develop a lot more discipline, rather than unnecessarily withdrawing when they feel they are being threatened. Easier said than done though, as it's the same behaviour the crab exhibits when under "duress!"

The alternating waves of extreme emotion, when put in check by Cancer folk, will help greatly in preventing them from conditions arising from excess water around the heart, eyes, and other parts of the body.

LEO

(July 23–Aug 22)

People born under the sign of Leo are inherently very strong, both physically and mentally, and are filled with a great sense of adventure, daring, and enthusiasm, so if they play the game of life properly, they are capable of attaining great heights!

After all, the symbol of this fifth sign of the zodiac is the incomparable king of the jungle – the lion! Whose thundering roar is a display of might, confidence, and fearlessness!

Continuing with this connection of traits, we all know a group of lions is called a pride. And interestingly enough, pride also just happens to be one of Leo's most dominant traits. Leos are endearing people, who love having company around. They are very gifted in telling a joke or a story and can really hold a crowd down. This is all very natural, though, as they enjoy being the center of attention.

Folks born under this sign are very affable and popular, which is quite understandable as they are so "free handed"— that it borders on the state of prodigality!

One of their weaknesses, though, is being too trusting, which makes them easy prey for the unscrupulous. And their lack of discrimination and inability to read character, leads to many unhappy relationships. Although this is more in the order of love affairs, rather than serious relationships, because of their promiscuous nature.

It is important for Leo folk to be masters of their own instincts and actions. Lest they fall prey to losing balance in their ever-so-vibrant personalities, and then their rich enthusiasm for life wanes and their inherent charisma just "withers" up.

The sign of Leo is ruled by the "heart" of the solar system – the sun, and like Leo's connections with the powerful lion, this association also shares a commonality. With Leos having a susceptibility to heart conditions and their attendant problems – high blood pressure and circulatory disorders!

VIRGO

(Aug 23–Sept 22)

Unlike the trait of discrimination that is not very pronounced in natives of Leo, we cannot say the same for those born under the sixth sign – Virgo.

Virgoans, because of their acute perception and subjecting everything to meticulous analysis, are able to choose the right path before them. And because of their ongoing commitment to their belief in high achievement, their diligence, and their careful attention to detail; it is not unusual that Virgoans are mostly successful!

Their adaptability serves them well too. As they are comfortable at both ends of the "table"– being a subordinate, or the head of the team.

Nevertheless, their critical nature sometimes leads them to be overly fussy and self-opinionated. And in always striving to be perfectionists, they may sometimes exhibit condescending and judgmental behavior.

Not falling into the category of being the most relaxed types, as well as the fact that this sign is governed by Mercury – controller of the nerves, Virgoans often suffer from hypertension and mental conditions.

Natives of this sign have a tendency to find themselves drawn to professions associated with the health field, and their critical nature serves them well when they seek out jobs where an analytic propensity is a prerequisite.

LIBRA

(Sep23–Oct 22)

Libra, the seventh sign, is ruled by Venus, hence people born under this sign are usually quite full of love. Not only this, but this connection may also strongly influence them to display a much purer form of this emotion. And mates of persons born under this sign can expect a display of a lot more conscientious, understanding, and unselfish behavior!

This richness of spirit apparently attunes them to a greater appreciation for the arts. And this leads them to have a keen interest in poetry, music, or painting.

The symbol of this sign is the balance. So maintaining balance becomes an important priority in the life of a Libran. And they will strive very hard to maintain peace and harmony in their interactions, so they will not have to be subjected, in the long run, to unnecessary worry and frustration.

Because of their mind-set, they become extremely selective in the type of vocation they pursue. And they may avoid many great opportunities, in which they could be successful. Mainly because they think the choice will be disruptive to the existing state of balance in their lives. To keep the peace (balance), they may oft-times refrain from getting involved in confrontations and will opt to turn their backs and walk away, rather than stay and face such disharmonious situations.

In having a predisposition not to easily make up their minds, it may not always be so easy for them to find an appropriate mate. Which can sometimes be troubling, as they become withdrawn, lonely, and depressed – a situation they try to resolve by getting overly dedicated to their careers.

Because of the unusual idiosyncrasies that Librans display, they are not easily understood, and may seem weak and cowardly, as the decisions they make do not always fit the criterion of what is considered logical.

If they cannot handle the emotional problems associated with loss of balance in situations, then they may suffer from complaints associated with the kidneys and bladder – areas of the body, that are governed by this sign.

SCORPIO

(Oct 23–Nov 21)

By its very influence, under Mars – the god of war, Scorpios tend to be strong-willed, forceful, charismatic, and have magnetic personalities. So much so, that they tend to command admiration and respect from those who know them well. And quite often, they even become a figurehead to some of those who look up to them. These traits serve Scorpios well, exemplifying the qualities that make them born leaders who are magnetic enough to be able to win over an audience.

When certain interests captivate the attention of a Scorpio, you can be assured he will go all-out to be most informed. And will then use this extensive acquired knowledge to make a positive influence in the lives of others. Peculiarly enough, though, they invariably keep their knowledge to themselves until they are quite sure they've mastered whatever it is they set out to learn.

However, natives born under this eighth-sign of the zodiac, display a very complex nature. One that exhibits a scale of extremes. For they can love with a great passion, and dislike with the "intensity" of the scorpion's sting (and finding it hard, to express any emotion in-between).

Moreover, it has been said that there are more saints and scoundrels born under this sign than under any other.

This hard-to-understand nature of the Scorpio native, can be attributed to the fact that this sign is uniquely represented by three symbols. Firstly, there is the scorpion, which can knowingly turn its venomous tail and bite itself. Then there is the serpent, which represents the birth of wisdom; and finally, the white eagle – the majestic bird that can soar to phenomenal heights above the thralldom of the phenomenal world, signifying the ultimate possibilities within reach for those born under this sign. Hence, it's not unusual for Scorpios to exhibit traits in their lives corresponding to what these three symbols represent.

The natives of this sign are full of creative ideas and have a natural knack for growing the financial resources of others – and should be given the opportunity to do so, more often than not.

Sexual energy is strongly associated with this sign. Scorpios are highly sexually charged people. And may be considered very uninhibited – willing to explore all possibilities, if they can.

However, if they can utilize this powerful energy for the higher good, like the awakening of the coiled-up kundalini serpent power. Then they tend to reach the heights aspired to by the eagle and awaken to the loftier realities. And that is why it is said that so many saints are born under this sign. For when they choose to aspire, it comes much easier to them, than to those born under other signs.

On the other hand, if they continuously fail to transmute this higher energy or do not find expression for it, then they may suffer from complications associated with the reproductive system and organs that have a connection with the elimination process, such as; the colon and rectum – all areas of the body with underlying, inherent weaknesses, from being born under this sign.

SAGGITARIUS

(Nov 22–Dec 21)

The personalities of those born under the ninth sign are characterized by a zest for life, a positive outlook, and having an upbeat rhythm to their step. Traits that make them quite popular, which is not so hard to picture – as they are delightful to be around and quite hospitable as well.

One is usually at ease in the presence of Sagittarians, as they make you feel like you've known them for most of your life.

Natives of this sign perceive life at a very deep level and display very inquiring minds; seeking to find answers to life's mysteries. Those with a strong Sagittarian influence have a high regard for morals and spiritual laws, and an unflinching respect for the principles of truth.

Their latent didactic tendencies may take root, as their exuberance to share their philosophies and visions become harder to contain. It's interesting too, that irrespective of their detours in life, they always have it at the back of their minds, what it is they're trying to achieve – never losing sight of their desired objectives!

Sagittarians are genuinely concerned about the welfare of others, and it usually doesn't take much for them to extend a helping hand to the less fortunate. Although they do sometimes feel disassociated from others who don't share their rich passion for life and may become judgmental. Nevertheless, this doesn't stop them from appreciating others for their intrinsic worth!

Those Sagittarians who do not capitalize on the inherent assets of their dual nature – being exceptionally strong both mentally and physically, will generally develop a genuine fondness for the outdoors – which usually includes a strong interest in travelling, as well. This is all connected to the influence of their birth sign, though, as it governs the limbs of locomotion.

In being so unselfish, dedicated, and extremely caring in showing their affection to their "companions," they may sometimes seem like pushovers, and become vulnerable to becoming easily taken advantage of by them!

It must be said Sagittarians are prone to self-indulgence, which plays a big part in the conditions they may have trouble from, associated with the pancreas and liver, as the planet Jupiter, which rules this sign, governs these organs.

CAPRICORN

(Dec 22–Jan 19)

Like the sure-footed mountain goat that rules Capricorn, natives born under the tenth sign also have their feet firmly planted on the ground. They are independent, introspective, and practical people, who usually set their aims pretty high. Despite the many challenges they may encounter, their patience and perseverance usually allow them to achieve whatever it is they try to attain!

This mould that Capricornians "come with," shapes them to have a keen interest in securing positions in management, as business executives and teachers, as well.

More often than not, Capricornians exude an air of dignity, importance and self-confidence, but they should take care that they do not tread on the toes of those, who they feel may not be their equals.

Regardless of their occasional shortcomings, it must be said that people do find them approachable, and enjoy their highly intellectual conversations. And it is not uncommon for many folks born under this sign to take up the fight for some worthy cause. The higher types of Capricornians may even begin to identify themselves with the feelings of humanity.

Capricorn natives do not attach themselves blindly to dogmas and belief systems, but seek out substantiation in what it is, they believe in. And if need be, they are willing to make the stringent sacrifices and adhere to the discipline required for them to get answers to the questions – they do seek!

On the health side of things, Capricorn governs the knees, bones and ligaments; and when natives of this sign stubbornly refuse to "bend their knees" with respect to their fixed way of thinking – then they may suffer from complaints like arthritis and rheumatism.

AQUARIUS

(Jan 20–Feb 18)

Man born under the eleventh sigh of the zodiac is beginning to feel a strong connection with the rest of humanity. He has finally reached the stage where he thinks there is no longer a need to keep proving to others how good he is. Pride has now taken a back step, and he silently goes about his business, trying to help others, and to make a difference where he can.

In fact, many of the higher types born under this sign turn out to be humanitarians; you may say it's like the water carrier (the symbol of this sign), possesses the water of life – which they can willingly share with those who are in need of a drink!

Aquarian folk can usually have quite sharp minds – which allow them to be innovative and creative. A point they should ponder though, is not to be totally preoccupied with what's going on in their heads, for then they may lose touch with reality, and end up being withdrawn and introverted. (That's not so unusual, though, for even in making friends, there are a lot of criteria for them to "work out,) before they really get close to you.)

Interestingly enough, although fortune and fame are not always foremost in their minds, nevertheless, if there is a special project that captivates their interest – then they step up to the plate and usually accomplish, extraordinary things!

Physiologically, if the "give and take" is missing in the life of an Aquarian, (which means the warmth of the heart energy is in short supply), then they may suffer from poor circulation and cool extremities; a connection related to the fact that the sign of Aquarius, is the ruler of the circulatory system.

PISCES

(Feb 19–Mar 20)

Finally, the twelfth sign of the zodiac is one that strongly signifies spiritualism, as represented by the symbol, two fishes, which in turn represent Him who became the Living Way – Lord Jesus! And it is a well-recognized fact that many born under this sign are highly evolved beings – known in everyday parlance as "old souls," who just have a little karma to work out. A fact that makes it easy to understand why Piceans have a natural gift to absorb knowledge, rather than having to "work hard," to retain it.

It is noteworthy to mention too, that the symbol of this sign is in many ways similar to the Yin-Yang principle, as one fish is moving upstream, and the other down. This is of significant relevance in the life of a Piscean, who has a strong force flowing through him. For if he loses control of it, and cannot utilize it for good, then he may turn to the vices of escapism, such as drugs, alcohol, and other excesses – knowing all the while that's not the direction his life should be taking.

Personally, folks born under this sign are attracted to fields that have a strong appeal to the spirit, such as poetry, painting, and music.

The planet Neptune, which governs this sign, also influences its natives to be involved in the healing professions and in the various branches of metaphysics.

It must be said that Pisceans are free spirits, who do not like to be hemmed in by rules, regulations, and restrictions, which instinctively make them very fond of travelling, and many also have an unusual fascination with the sea – most likely, because Neptune – is strongly associated with the same.

A rather unique trait shared by these folks is that, they are hopeless romantics, who have the endearing quality of not forgetting the little surprises in life that make their dear ones, exceedingly happy.

Those Pisceans who have a tendency to keep their emotions all pent up, may suffer from complications related to the lymphatic system, due to the fact, that Jupiter (another planet that governs this sign), governs this system also.

EXCEPTIONS TO THE RULE

In as much as each sign of the zodiac will give a general depiction of what its natives will "be like," nevertheless, when we consider several hundred million people taking birth under each sign, it's hardly likely that they all will fit the mould exactly.

As is obvious, each one possesses his own idiosyncrasies. Nevertheless, the pure types born under each sign will, more often than not, fit the model more realistically. That is those having birthdays a few days after the previous zodiacal sign, and also a few days before the next commences. As no doubt, there will be less of an overlapping influence, from these neighbouring signs.

IT'S A STARRY, STARRY LIFE

Unperceived by our mind's eye;
Or unaware of, in our mortal consciousness,
And even a little mind-boggling,
To fully comprehend!
That, that which decorates the firmament,
That, that which seems so insignificant,
That, that which is regarded
By a mere handful
For its aesthetic value—
The celestial bodies in the majestic firmament.

Depict a mysterious, symbolic map
In its utmostly precise configuration,
At the time of birth.
Of our inherent traits, future disposition,
And give us, a crystal ball view,
Into the future events,
In one's life.
Especially those, when
Ground-breaking events occur!

CHAPTER 9 | # The Seven Inner Serpents

 If ever there was an empire that was the epitome of pomp and ceremony, we need look no further than the glory days of the Mogul empire in India, under the rule of the renowned emperor, Aurangzeb, whose golden reign lasted from 1658–1707. To match, he exacted the almost incredible annual tribute of over thirty-eight million pounds in 1690.

In as much as this information speaks of awe and fascination, nonetheless, it is the treachery and ruthlessness he utilized in attaining the Peacock Throne that is of relevance to the topic of this chapter.

Being the third of four sons, it is obvious he was not favored to inherit the throne. So, although he enjoyed the luxuries and conveniences of the princely life, (as he held official positions in the kingdom), because of greed, he was viciously propelled to imprison his ailing father, the king – Shah Jahan, (who is best remembered for building the fourth wonder of the world – the Taj Mahal); and in the most evil and unscrupulous way – had his brothers – "disposed of!"

We find all religions of the world have emphatically pointed out that "to have" greed in our nature is an evil that surely will keep us at a distance from our creator! As this quote from the Bible aptly testifies: "And thou hast greedily gained of thy neighbours by extortion and hast forgotten me, saith the Lord God."[92]

Along with this, there are six other qualities also included in the world scriptures, which are referred to as clear-cut instruments that will surely put a spoke in our wheel on our journey to realization of our relationship with Him who created us!

In this chapter, they will be referred to as – the seven inner serpents! And they are as follows; greed, gluttony, lust, anger, pride, sloth, and envy. Which many moviegoers may recall as the seven deadly sins, from the box office bonanza – the movie *Seven,* from 1995.

GREED

Introspectively, it can easily be deduced that any trait one may possess that can instigate one to take a life, can definitely be referred to as being not righteous, but extremely evil. As it is common knowledge: that the Sixth Commandment adamantly points out: "Thou shalt not kill!"[93]

Looking at the big picture, however, it's only because of man's magnetic attraction to the phenomenal world, that this inner serpent is allowed to raise its evil head. For it's when we possess unresolved desires that greed is allowed to manifest in our being. In this regard then, when we have this trait in our nature, without a doubt there will be nary a chance of realizing our true identities, as we will be utterly distracted from ever finding the truth within, in much the same way as a starry-eyed lover will be distracted by having, eyes for another!

This second quotation from the Bible corroborates the fact that when this serpent is entwined around us, it will keep us in the spiritual doldrums. "[Those] who being past feeling have given themselves over unto lasciviousness, to work all uncleanness with greediness."[94]

GLUTTONY

Although this serpent is literally as well, greed (but in this instance being an unquenchable desire for food and drink). It nevertheless is more or less generally alluded to as the serpent – gluttony.

Physiologically this trait is rather unhealthy, for it has scientifically been proven to contribute to many illnesses. And in light of the fact that body and mind work together, it becomes fully evident that an ailing body will leave little room for a mind-set to investigate the deeper mysteries of life!

But even more importantly, it creates a state that induces restless thoughts. And is therefore a great hindrance to us in having a calm mind, which makes the journey inward to reconnect with our divine self – the soul, almost an impossibility.

In many instances, this serpent controls us, because the flesh is weak (although as the Bible says, the spirit is willing).[95] And usually when this is the case, it is not that easy to follow the principles and ideals of spiritualism that lead to self-realization, for one is most likely totally caught up in the material world, easily developing more delusion-leading habits, due to absorption in what the ego finds pleasurable.

This inner serpent brings about also, blockages to the chakras, so even one who is trying to find his true self through meditation and contemplation and is not rid of this undesirable quality, will find progress to be a colossal challenge, as it will definitely keep his soul, body-conscious, (because as already mentioned), it is the awakening of the chakras that leads to inner illumination.

It is hard to develop then, earnest devotion to God, when one's deity becomes what will be placed before him for the next meal, even before completing the one, set before him.

In other words, you might say, he who lives to eat will find it impossible to live to find God!

---

95   Mark 14:38.

LUST

It would seem, rather, that the inner serpents are like chameleons, for in instances, the interchangeability of their traits, (as seen with greed and gluttony), seems as natural as it is for the real creatures to undergo metamorphosis.

For here again, we find lust means an insatiable desire for money and power (almost the same as greed), however, in addition it also includes an insatiable desire for sex. And it is this latter meaning, that is of concern to us.

This inner serpent, when looked at from the deepest level, will be revealed as one of the most soul-detracting, for as already pointed out, the sex impulse was implanted in us solely for the purpose of procreation. And having already fallen from grace (into sin), by succumbing to procreation by physical means, instead of immaculate conception. To utilize this inherent sex impulse almost exclusively for self-gratification (succumbing to the inner serpent of lust), can only mean that we are headed down a road that takes us even further away, from our spiritual heritage.

Then again, it is highly unlikely that one seeking out a steady stream of "partners" will find the time to discover that he has a divine nature.

On the metaphysical front, when a man leaves the phenomenal world with lust still firmly embedded in his consciousness. Regrettably, he can only satisfy his insatiable desire by returning to the earth plane; the gross realm of duality (home of pain, sorrow and suffering) – the only place, where material desires can be fulfilled!

These two Biblical quotes are ample proof that this inner serpent of lust is not of our true nature, but belongs to the fleshy, temporal overcoat of the body. (And one even gives credence to the fact that part of us is eternal). "Dearly beloved, I beseech you as strangers and pilgrims, abstain from fleshy lusts, which war against the soul."[96] And: "For all that is in the world, the lust of the flesh ... is not of the Father, but is of the world.

---

96   1 Peter 2:11.

And the world passeth away, and the lust thereof, but he that doeth the will of God abideth forever!"[97]

ANGER

This inner serpent, no doubt, is one which most of us can identify with, more or less, quite solidly. Maybe not so much as to how it prevents us from something as profound as realizing we are made in the image of the Divine. But rather, that when it "wraps itself" around us we are aware that we behave in a manner that is quite uncharacteristic of ourselves.

With regards to the latter, we know when anger (or wrath as it is more commonly referred to in the scriptures) is "stirred up" within us, we feel a great welling up of heat in our brains; we lose control of ourselves. It affects our judgement and peace of mind, and robs us of the ability to think logically. All of which, is out of sync with what's inherent in the spark of divinity that exists within us.

In this condition we are propelled to perform evil acts, which create negative karma and keep us in delusion, even further.

And in this state also, it's hardly likely that we would be in a frame of mind for contemplation of the Divine.

In fact, the effect of being under the sway of this serpent is so deleterious, that it even leads to deterioration of the nerves, as well as to the secretion of poisons within our systems. (Lasting control by this serpent, in fact, may ultimately lead to the complete burning out of the nerves).

Very interestingly, numerous experiments have been carried out on people possessed by wrath, and it has been found that its caustic effect is so powerful that the venom found on their tongues is not that different from that found on a serpent's.

A somewhat similar experiment concluded that the analysis of an enraged person's breath revealed it contained enough poison in it to render a small rodent lifeless!

---

97   1 John 2:16, 17.

Substantiation of how this serpent affects the mind and keeps us in delusion, (as discussed above), can be found in this verse from the Bhagavad Gita: "From anger, complete delusion arises and from delusion bewilderment of memory. When memory is bewildered, intelligence is lost, and when intelligence is lost one falls down again into the material pool."[98]

Taking a closer and deeper look at the bigger picture, however, will reveal to us a view that should make it a little easier to understand how this serpent affects us from realizing who we really are.

No doubt, many are familiar with Christ's pacific proclamation that: If someone strikes thee on one cheek, we should turn the other![99] A statement which can only seem logical when interpreted from scriptural teachings of the deepest metaphysical level, which proclaim all men are made in the image of God. In this sense, then, when we become enraged with someone, it means we are still living in delusion, believing ourselves to be different and separate from our fellow man. For in reality, we are actually directing our anger at the Divine presence within another. Which in essence means that our "venom" is aimed only at ourselves!

Only on the acknowledgement of this teaching too, can the not-so-easily-understood reply Jesus voiced to Peter when he asked, "Lord, how oft shall my brother sin against me, and I forgive him? Till seven times?" seem quite comprehensible. Which was, "I say not unto thee, until seven times, but until seventy times seven."[100]

Indeed, having forbearance is a spiritual quality worthy striving for, as per this Biblical quote, which acclaims it to be more worthy than being in possession of great power: "He that is slow to anger is better than the mighty; and he that ruleth his spirit than he that taketh a city."[101] The latter indicating as well what we are capable of when we rid ourselves of all inner serpents and live in accordance with divine principles!

---

98   II:63.
99   Luke 6:29.
100   Matt. 18:21, 22.
101   Prov. 16:32.

PRIDE

As to why having this venomous serpent in our nature seems discordant to our true being, may pose to be quite baffling, indeed. But like most of the others in the "family," it's only when viewed from the highest metaphysical level can there seem to be any logic, why this is so!

But firstly, though, this abridged and enlightening narrative should prove to be quite an incisive introduction.

As already mentioned in chapter five, the deathless[102] avatar Babaji, materialized a palace for his very special disciple, Lahiri Mahashaya. However, it was no ordinary palace, as it was completely created from solid gold. The interior was inlaid with the most wondrous precious stones, and the throne upon which the master sat to welcome his devotee was a wonder in itself too, as it was made of the finest gold, and encrusted with innumerable, exquisite jewels.

One would naturally think that someone with the power to create kingdoms of untold wealth at his fingertips would be all swelled up with great pride.

But quite the contrary, for when the disciple ran into his master on another occasion; at the great religious festival that occurs periodically in India – the Khumba Mela, Babaji was seen washing the feet of an anchorite, (and later on, he did other menial tasks, like cleaning his cooking utensils, as well). On witnessing the highly unusual encounter, the disciple was, no doubt, exceedingly surprised. It was then that the master understandingly glanced at him and said, "The greatest of virtues pleasing to God above all others, is humility."

The special quality of this trait is further expounded in the Bible, which states: "Who [he] humbleth himself to behold the things that are in

---

102   The avatar, who is already several centuries old, will remain in physical form, as long as there are humans on the planet. See *Autobiography of a Yogi*, chapter thirty-three.

heaven and in the earth."[103] And again it says: "Whosoever shalt exalt himself shall be abased and he that shall humble himself shall be exalted."[104]

It should be of interest to note that this inner serpent only becomes part of our nature when we identify ourselves with the material world. For when we do so, we shut out God's light, thinking ourselves to be the temporary, perishable casing – called the body, (owing to the soul being totally "bound up," as the ego). When in fact, being the "Sons of the Most High," no matter how great our earthly possessions might be, they are in no way comparable to the infinite riches that are already ours.

Another aspect that displays how pride is not in harmony with our true nature is easily revealed when we realize that the eternal soul is one and the same, in each. For then we learn that there is no reason why we should want to feel more important and superior to others, and want to lord it over them.

In fact, knowing as we do that humbleness was found in abundance in the self-realized masters that walked the earth (such as Lord Jesus, who was a carpenter, and the enlightened One – the Buddha – the prince, who gave up everything, and became a complete renunciant) should be reason enough to believe that the development of this trait is something worth striving for.

Isn't it quite ironical, though, how when trials and tribulations befall us, our arrogance and pride somehow shift into the background as we realize how helpless and vulnerable we are, as we meekly and subserviently turn to a Higher Power seeking solace, guidance, and strength?

It would be wise to remember too, that material possessions are only temporary gifts borrowed from He who created them, and there is no guarantee that we may be fortunate enough to be as prosperous and secure as we are in this life, in the next! Also, our haughtiness and other negative attitudes associated with this venomous serpent, more often

103   Psalms 113:6.
104   Matt. 23:12.

than not, only create more negative karma, which ultimately leads us down the path, to further delusion.

This Biblical reference that says: Pride is evil and indicates, that it defileth the man, actually sums up this serpent's venomous nature quite nicely: "Thefts, covetousness, wickedness, deceit, lasciviousness, an evil eye, blasphemy, pride, foolishness: All these evil things come from within, and defile the man."[105]

SLOTH

By its very nature, being contrary to creation that is perpetually in motion, this inner serpent that makes us prone to chronic inactivity, should be considered no less, than an insult and degradation to the divine spark that exists within. After all, the Bhagavad Gita proclaims: "Perform your prescribed duty, for doing so is better than not working. One cannot even maintain one's physical body without work."[106]

For each and every man plays a part in God's divine play (lila). And no matter how small or insignificant it may be, it nevertheless contributes to the successful unfoldment of his divine production.

And to not participate in it, is to stifle the soul – for each of our actions is part of the ever-so-gradual process in the evolution of the wave (the soul), toward mergence with the Ocean (the Creator). When we consider that we ourselves have chosen the role we play, selected in the astral world with the purpose of learning a specific lesson, and strongly influenced by our karmic blueprint. It becomes all that much clearer why we should rid ourselves of this serpent.

To think too that we all possess a vast potential within us, as divine will, and not even attempt to use it cannot be considered to be much other than a sacrilege to who we really are.

---

105   Mark 7:22-23
106   III:8.

It's no wonder then that the Bible likens the presence of this serpent to the dire situation of having life itself, "expelled" from the body.[107]

The elucidation of the above subject would be incomplete, however, if some misconceptions were not quelled with regards to those who sit in isolation, away from society amidst the Himalayan peaks and secluded cavernous retreats in constant contemplation and meditation, seemingly in a state of complete inertia.

Solitude, however, is a prerequisite for one striving to accelerate the process, to realize the purpose for which he was created. And when he makes extreme strides (man to God), his thoughts and holy vibrations bestow more benefits on the world than can ever be possibly imagined!

ENVY

*"A sound heart is the life of the flesh
but envy the rottenness of the bones!"*[108]

Again, in this case, (like some others), when this serpent raises its deadly head, it prevents us from seeing unity in creation, and feeling separateness, we begin to view others as being better off financially, having more possessions, and being superior to ourselves.

Indeed, if we have learned our spiritual lessons, we would know that the seeming inequality in men is not God's creation, for we are all made in His image, (and therefore equal). So there should be no justification for us to begrudge others of their good fortune – they've genuinely earned it – fruits of their past karma.

This serpent makes identifying with the ego even stronger, that is; identifying with the temporal body and its traits and personality, and less with the immortal soul. Hence, it should be easy to see why this serpent impedes our progress toward spiritual perfection.

---

107 "The desire of the slothful killeth him; for his hands refuse to labour" (Prov.21:25).
108 Proverbs 14:30.

It's rather ironic, though, that although many may consider themselves to be very religious and living an ideal moral life, if they still have this serpent coiled around them, it may be a case of self-deception for they are openly transgressing one of God's most powerful commandments, found in every major scriptural text, (worded in some form or the other); "Love thy neighbor as thyself." It is evident then, that the oil of their devotion is surely not mixing with the pure water of their spiritual teaching.

As a matter of fact, it would be rather much more spiritually rewarding if they could channel this negative "energy" into being more compassionate and of selfless service to the less fortunate, and most of all – "shed" love. For love is the essence of the Unmanifested Absolute!

The delusionary nature of this serpent is best summed up by this quote from the Gita: "Those persons who execute their duties according to My injunctions and who follow this teaching[109] faithfully, without envy, become free from the bondage of fruitive actions. But those who, out of envy, disregard these teachings and do not follow them are to be considered bereft of all knowledge, befooled, and ruined in their endeavours for perfection."[110]

PUTTING IT ALL TOGETHER

Man will easily see his connection with the Creator when he is able to rid himself of all seven deadly serpents. As he will lose the delusionary feeling of separateness and intuitively feel his connection with all life. Which will ultimately lead to the realization that he is not the body, but the divine spark, within.

At the same time, though, (as this quote will show), it is wise to remember there are definitely some who are more venomous than others, (although, as we know), even a little venom, can cause great harm. "There

109 The edification taking place between Lord Krishna and his disciple Arjuna, throughout the volume.
110 III:31, 32.

are three gates leading to ... hell – lust, anger, and greed. Every sane man should give these up, for they lead to the degradation of the soul."[111]

In closing, the next quote – a conversation between the disciple Arjuna and Lord Krishna, should answer one of the most perplexing questions to enter the human mind. Arjuna quizzically asks, "By what is one impelled to sinful acts, even unwillingly, as if engaged by force?"

And the Supreme Personality of Godhead replies, "It is lust[112] only, Arjuna, which is born of contact with the material mode of passion and later transformed into wrath, and which is the all-devouring sinful enemy of the world."[113]

In other words, anger raises its deadly head when we are prevented from acquiring the desires of our lust. And as a result, this leads to loss of control of our will power. And, as we know, this usually leads us to say and do things that we may regret later, again creating a lot of unnecessary karma.

By no stretch of the imagination, however, should one consider ridding oneself of these serpents, to be – a stroll in the park.

---

111 XVI:21.
112 Lust here covers the whole spectrum; the insatiable desire for sex, money and power!
113 III:36, 37.

THE SEVEN INNER SERPENTS

Put to rest all vanity—
The absence of pride,
That humbleth the man—
That maketh him,
As endearing and guileless,
Like the endearing child.

Put to flight, the mighty ego!
Arresting the uncontrollable desire
For Power, Wealth, and Fame!
And close the inviting doors
To the soul stifling serpents of
Anger, Envy, and Greed,
Upon which our beguiling ego feeds.

Stir the inherent "motor of action,"
To "squash" the divine will—
Impeding serpent, Sloth.
But use soul-guiding conscience
And wise judgement,
Not to get lost in tempting Lust;
Nor to overburden the divine soul within
With the insatiable craving
For food and drink (greed),
Two other deadly serpents,
That will surely lead us—
To the delusional brink!

CHAPTER 10

The Yugas

 From the fascinating world of Oriental astronomy, a science advanced thousands of years before discovered by the Occident, which elucidates complex concepts like; the way planetary bodies move in a heliocentric motion in the solar system; the Milky Way having fixed stars in its galaxy; the moon's luminosity, being a result of a reflection and many others.[114] We learn of the very interesting pathway of the life-giving sun, which is of relevance to this chapter.

As is quite commonly known, the planets are continually rotating about their axes and having moons rotating about them. And in turn, this entire complex system of bodies simultaneously rotates around the sun. But what may not be so familiar is the incredible journey, the sun undertakes.

In the first instance, it takes some star for its dual, and in the lengthy period of 24,000 years, makes a complete revolution around it, causing the backward movement of the equinoctial points around the zodiac. But more importantly, it also rotates around another fixed body of much greater relevance – called Vishnunabhi – (a divine heavenly body) – also known as the seat of Brahma; that is an influencing factor of spirituality in man's consciousness.

---

114   From Jyotish: a section of the Vedas that deals with astronomical expositions.

At the time when the sun is nearest to this center, which occurs when the Autumnal equinox touches upon the first point of the zodiacal body – Aries, a spiritual renaissance occurs that allows the majority of humans to comprehend all of the Creator's secrets, even the mystifying hidden workings of the Father beyond creation. Peace and harmony reign supreme, and man finally lives the ideal of feeling brotherhood, with his fellow man – as he clearly discerns the divine spark to be in all.

This signals the beginning of what is known as Satya Yuga, or the Golden Age, which lasts for a period of 4,800 years.

Following this age, with the sun's continual movement away from Vishnunabhi, the earth passes through three more distinct Yugas.

The next being, Treta Yuga (the Silver Age), which lasts for a period of 3,600 years.

During this time, man's ability to comprehend spiritual matters continually declines. And even his ability to grasp profound scientific principles like divine magnetism – that nullify the concept of time, slowly ebbs away.

Following this, we have the Dwapara Yuga (the Bronze Age), which has a duration of 2,400 years, and as might be expected, mankind's intellect becomes more entwined with the fabric of materialism. And his understanding of complex scientific principles declines even further. As he experiences a diminishing ability to comprehend electricities and their attributes – which are the not-so-visible foundations of the phenomenal world.

In the age of Kali (the Iron Age) – the last of the cycles – which lasts for 1,200 years. (And isn't it wonderful that its duration falls short of the more illuminating ages?). We arrive at a time, (which begins when the Autumnal Equinox crosses the first point of Libra and because the sun is furthest away from Vishnunabhi), when man has retrogressed to the lowest standards in society – one void of every trace of spiritualism. Not to mention that his intellect is hardly able to conceptualize anything beyond the gross physical creation.

Thus concludes, at the end of a 12,000 year period, four Yugas, known as a Daiva Yuga or Electric Couple, in which the former are said to occur in a descending arc, as the sun's orbit continually moves away from the seat of Brahma—Vishnunabhi.

It is of relevance too, to point out that although the Yugas have fixed durations, that during that span of time there is also a fixed number of years preceding and succeeding each Yuga, called a mutation period or sandhi. Whereby the influences of the "connecting" Yugas mildly interplay with each other as one age meshes into another. In the case of the Kali Yuga, which has a duration of 1,200 years, it has a mutation period of a hundred years before the actual Yuga, and a hundred years of mutation at the end of the cycle; with these years being included in the 1,200-year duration of the age of Kali.[115]

As the sun begins the reverse process, the four Yugas repeat themselves, (and one might say, a great reprieve; the worst is over for at least several thousand years), for with every movement the sun makes in an ascending arc toward Vishnunabhi, man gradually regains his ability to comprehend the mysteries in God's creation. That is; he becomes more enlightened, and spiritually inclined.

This concludes another Daiva Yuga of 12,000 years. Or a complete rotation around the divine center in 24,000 years – known as an Electric Cycle.

For the first 1,200 years, in what is now the ascending Kali Yuga (the "Material" or Iron age), man's intellect gradually regains familiarity with the very basic things of a scientific nature.

And although there are usually no major changes in the intense unrest in the various kingdoms, it can be said there is usually no further deterioration in animosities!

Following this, the ascending Dwapara Yuga, which lasts 2,400 years begins and brings with it a much greater understanding of scientific principles, and man is now able to unravel in an enormous way, the principles behind the functioning of electricity and its attributes. A large field

---

115 In the case of the Dwapara, Treta, and Satya Yugas, they have mutation periods before and after of 200, 300, and 400 years respectively – included also in the duration of their cycles.

indeed, for just as there are five unique types of electricities, as transmitted through the five sensory nerves associated with our hearing, touch, sight, taste, and smell, there are also five related types of electricities found in the external world. (For example: the sight-giving optic nerve only transmits light, and the auditory nerve only sound, and aren't able to interchange their functions).

As part of the evolution of knowledge in this age, treatment and healing of diseases are carried out more and more by the use of rays. After all, it's rather a much more effective healing approach than other methods in that this form of energy can target the electronic forces of atoms much more easily and effectively than the much cruder form of chemicals, can.

And lastly, this is the age in which travelling by air becomes a reality. With greater and greater advances made in this field as the age progresses.

As might be expected, next ushers in the ascending Treta Yuga, which lasts 3,600 years. In which there is now an even greater conception of the mystical forces of creation – like divine magnetism – the force behind all electrical phenomena. And being the mental age, the majority of mankind will use their highly advanced mental ability to accomplish seemingly impossible feats like communicating telepathically, healing the body of its illnesses, and sustaining it by drawing prana or life energy through the medulla oblongata[116] (connected by polarity to the sixth chakra), instead of dependence on gross foods for its sustenance. The last being a technique employed by highly advanced yogis throughout the "ages," and one mentioned in chapter forty-six of *Autobiography of a Yogi*. A narrative in which a divine being materialized and imparted the sacred technique to someone trying to resolve a critical problem in their life. And from that moment on, no longer found it necessary to consume food or water, for nourishment.

---

116 "Man shall not live by bread alone, but by every word that proceedeth out of the mouth of God" (Matthew 4:4). Meaning; Man cannot live by the things he eats alone, but the prana (cosmic energy) which enters the medulla oblongata is far more essential to his sustenance than the former; Paramahansaji's interpretation. In chapter fourteen, it will become much clearer: the connection between "word" and prana.

Concluding the ascending Daiva Yuga or Electric Couple, is the illuminating Golden Age or Satya Yuga of 4,800 years – which is the best time to be incarnated. As mankind's actions are effortlessly coordinated with the divine plan – which means there is no longer a feeling of separateness, but rather being of the same essence. And their elevated consciousness can penetrate to the core of the deepest spiritual truths, to unravel all their profoundest secrets, even those about – Eternal Spirit, beyond the physical world!

In this environment then, it occurs that many human beings become fully realized!

Even the what-may-seem-impossible feat of entering the astral planes and making contact with and communicating with souls who were once close – becomes a reality for many human beings.

Well, one may well wonder, how actual events play out with respect to those expected to take place during a particular Yuga.

To do this, it would be prudent as well as convenient to start in the year 701 B.C. – the beginning of the last descending Kali Yuga. Signalling the darkest time on the planet, in the entire 24,000 year period of the sun's revolution around the seat of Brahma. As then, it is much easier to corroborate actual events with those in recorded history.

Without going into detail, it is well-documented that in this sinister period from 701 B.C. to 499 A.D. – (Age of Kali), the world was indeed in a state of utter chaos and backwardness, and indeed it was a time void of any semblance of spiritualism; as paganism and atheism were the predominant flavors of the day.

It should be no wonder then, that both the enlightened one – the Buddha, and the divine Christ chose to "come down" during this extremely crucial period in the earth's history! "Whenever and wherever there is a decline in religious practice, O descendant of Bharata (Arjuna), and a predominant rise of irreligion – at that time I descend Myself."[117]

---

117   Bhagavad Gita IV:7. Lord Krishna giving divine instruction to his disciple – Arjuna.

Moving to the next age, from 499 A.D. to 1,699 A.D., which is now the reverse process (the ascending Kali Yuga), there was still not much to "cheer about," excepting that there was a gradual upliftment of man's intellect from being at the bottom of the barrel to what may be considered an improvement over its previous state, and a slight easing of warring among each other.

Before a comparison is made in what has elapsed of the next period, from 1,699 to 4,099 A.D. in what is the ascending Dwapara Yuga, it should be pointed out that there is a discrepancy and error, with some sources labelling the present time as still a continuation of the descending Kali Yuga, with several hundred thousand years, still to come.

An error that appeared in the Hindu almanacs around 702 B.C., just about the time before the dawning of the descending Kali Yuga.

Knowing that this dark period was about to occur, the reigning Maharaja[118] of that time – Yudhisthira, "turned over" the kingdom to his grandson – Parikshit, and headed off to the secluded Himalayan retreats with his holy and learned men, to dedicate the remaining years of their lives to spiritual practices.

Thus, with the arrival of the period (a year later), that signaled the decline of knowledge, and with the absence of the wise men in the court, the people left in charge could not figure out the duration of the Yugas, and so without numbering the year as one at the commencement of this Yuga, they simply added one to the 2,400 year duration of the descending Dwapara Yuga. Or in other words, the first year of the Kali Yuga was numbered as being in the 2,401th year.[119]

---

118 "Great king"– a title of respect.

119 Skilled astronomers can easily corroborate this miscalculation by pinpointing when the sun is farthest away from Vishnunabhi, that is when the Vernal (opposite of Autumnal) Equinox comes to the first point of Aries. They can then measure how far the Vernal Equinox has regressed from this point and can then translate this figure (by calculation) into years. Hence knowing how many years have elapsed since the occurrence of this event. Currently, in the year 2020, 1520 years have elapsed. Deducting 1,200 years for the period of the ascending Kali Yuga, it thus reveals we are at this time in the 320th year of the ascending Dwapara Yuga.

As time went by and the intellect of the men of the society slowly improved, the mistake was eventually detected. However, in trying to rectify the problem, they only made the situation worse. As still yet not fully enlightened in matters of astronomy, (because of the period they were in); they erroneously numbered the 1,200-year duration of the Kali Yuga as being in "years of the Gods" – (one "God" year being the equivalent of 360 years here on earth). Hence giving the Kali Yuga the duration of 432,000 years and still having several hundred thousand years to run before the transition into the Dwapara Yuga; the current age – we are actually in.

Returning to the age at hand; the changes we expect to see in the Dwapara Yuga already started to occur in the hundred-year transition period (sandhi)[120] of the ascending Kali Yuga, as it flowed into this "cycle." To recount some of the many outstanding contributions in the scientific world; around 1600 William Gilbert was instrumental in getting the "ball rolling" with his discovery of magnetic forces and his bringing to light the presence of electricity in material things! In 1608, the German, Hans Lippershey, invented the telescope. And in 1687, Sir Isaac Newton "gave us" his three laws of motion, which contributed greatly in the advancement of the field of physics. (Not to underplay his other major contributions in the field or in other disciplines, as well.)

Honorary mention should be made too, of Thomas Savery, who invented the steam powered engine in 1698; which played a major part in sustaining the momentum of the Industrial Revolution.[121]

And although unrest still remained widespread, there were still positive changes in some parts of the world. In Europe, after centuries of feuding and chicanery, England united with Scotland in 1707. While the great emperor Napoleon introduced his legal code in France in 1804, giving the "common man," a lot more rights and freedom! And on another

---

120   Around 1599 –1699 A. D.

121   The name given to the period of rapid expansion in industry, in England, (late eighteenth and early nineteenth century); and later spreading to other lands.

continent, the bitter civil war in America had come to an end, after the country finally gained recognition of its independence, in 1776.

It should be pointed out, though, that although "fine matters" were brought into practical use in so many diverse fields and contributed to so many technological advancements, their nature was not yet fully understood.

It was not until after 1899, when the two hundred years of the mutation period of the ascending Dwapara Yuga had elapsed, that there was a comprehensive understanding of these electricities, and their attributes.

In view of this then, it is no surprise that the unprecedented advancements in what the Western world innovatively refers to as the Atomic Age, and the Age of Aviation, coincided with this transition.

As a continuation of this wave of technological expansion, we are now experiencing the internet revolution, which started a few decades ago and shows no sign of letting up. And there are also signs indicating that with the barriers to space being more and more dismantled, it shouldn't be long before there are almost no limits to interstellar travel.

While on the other hand, although it seems there is no end to large-scale warfare, the silver lining is; learning to live in harmony will gradually improve, instead of "going the other way!"

THE REALITY OF IT ALL

In view of the characteristic nature of the Yugas, it should be more of an eye-opener as to why the secrets of creation continue to be a grand mystery to us. For without being aware of it, the age in which we choose to "take birth," influences, to a large extent, the depth of knowledge we can actually comprehend.

In light of this powerful macrocosmical influence that so drastically affects us, it's not that the amazing claims made by avatars, self-realized masters, and scriptural texts that we are made in the image of God, and the purpose of human life is to reunite with the Creator sound very incredible. But rather, that our vitiated consciousness (caused by the age we're born in), cannot assimilate such profound, soul-awakening knowledge, even if we are exposed to it!

However, it's reassuring to know that not everyone is affected, but mainly a predominant part of humanity. For in the world of duality, it's very unnatural that everyone would have the same mind-set.

Nevertheless, although we are in the Dwapara Yuga (the electrical age), it doesn't mean we cannot find the truth, but it just means our search has to be intensified and our open mindedness must be – a lot more flexible.

For these timeless truths are always available, just waiting to be discovered by earnest seekers trying to unravel the perplexing nature of human life. And as incredible as it may sound, there are always "God-men" ready to enlighten us, irrespective of what Yuga, we find ourselves incarnated in!

THE YUGAS

Kali, Dwapara, Tretya, Satya Yuga;
Whatever Age fate has decreed,
That I incarnate in
I will by the divine power within me:
That the time of birth
Will scarce have an effect on me.
That it will shed no blanket over me,
To burden me further,
In trying to "unloose" that innateness,
Which is not mortal,
But instead is—
Eternal, Omnipresent Spirit!

CHAPTER 11 | Beyond The Realm of The Norm

It is the objective of this chapter in no small way; by the cases cited, the facts mentioned, and the displays of wonderment that these illustrations of a phenomenal nature indicate that man has at his disposal capabilities well beyond the realm of logic, which cannot be attributed to him being merely a physical entity, but rather, that he indeed has an inherent, divine nature.

SOME SCIENTIFIC FACTS

To investigate the cause of the phenomenon of transcendental meditation, which was creating waves in the sixties and early seventies, scientists conducted numerous experiments. Their results were indeed amazing (as mentioned in chapter two).

One of their most astonishing findings was that the state of rest achieved during a meditator's twenty-minute practice[122] was almost double the state that we achieve – when we are most rested, during deep sleep. An experiment[123] easily conducted by measuring oxygen consumption

---

122   The practice entails: two twenty-minute sessions daily.

123   Excerpt from: *TM Discovering Inner Energy and Overcoming Stress* by H. H. Bloomfield, M.P. Cain, D. T. Jaffe, and R.B. Kory; pages 91-95. New York, N.Y: Dell Publishing.

through a mask worn over the lower face. A reading that gives how rested we are. For as is common knowledge; the more restful we become, the slower our rate of breathing and hence, the less oxygen, we take in.

But topping their list of findings was the fact that meditators experience a new and distinct state of consciousness unknown to the "common man."

With electrodes attached to the scalp and analyzing the electrical activity of the surface of the brain, it has been established that the "average" person only experiences three states of consciousness; waking, sleeping and dreaming – each giving a characteristic pattern, indicating the state we're in. For example, when we are dreaming, also known as REM sleep, delta waves are emitted. But when the test was conducted on people practicing the transcendental meditation technique, an unknown, uncharacteristic wave pattern showed up on the electroencephalograph – the ultrasensitive apparatus that gives readings of the brain waves, indicating the meditators were "accessing" a fourth state of consciousness![124]

Although not verified by scientific analysis, even more remarkable than this finding is that the guru of the transcendental meditation movement – Sri Maharishi Yogi has pronounced that, "As meditators progress in their practice through the years – they achieve even higher states of consciousness!"

AN EVEN MUCH DEEPER STATE OF REST

In the world of scientific meditation there are numerous techniques, and it is through some of the most advanced techniques that the spiritual masters are able to perform the remarkable feats that we have heard so many incredible stories about, like yogis being buried alive for many days at a time and showing no adverse effects after their disinterment.

In as much as this sounds farfetched, there is a scientific basis; a state of slowing down the heartbeat to its "quietest levels," that allows for the accomplishing of such miraculous feats.

---

124   See: *TM Discovering Inner Energy and Overcoming Stress*, page 113.

For in much the same way as the transcendental meditation technique brings about a dramatic decline in oxygen consumption (a lower breathing rate), as a result of a significant slowing down of the body's metabolic process, at the cellular level. Practitioners of these higher techniques, who spend many hours in daily meditation, and who live only on pure foods (that produce hardly any waste in the body), can reproduce these states at the extreme levels! In bringing the metabolic activity in their bodies down to such low levels, continuous cell breakdown of the muscles and tissues is completely arrested. Consequently, there is no need for the overworked heart to pump carbon dioxide-laden blood (a by-product of cellular breakdown), to the lungs, for "cleaning." Nor is there a necessity for the heart to pump freshly inhaled oxygen (attached to molecules of hemoglobin in the blood), to feed the bodily tissues. Thus resulting in the heart attaining a very deep state of rest. Also, without no need for oxygen, breathing simply becomes unnecessary. A requirement for being buried alive! A state in which the yogis can simply exist on excess cosmic energy stored in the brain and spinal column, and one not too different than that in which animals exist when they are in suspended animation.

Now that the theory behind the "deathless state" has been explained, here are examples of three spiritual masters who could have gone into this ecstatic state.

In his book *Mejda: The Family and the Early Life Of Paramahansa Yogananda,*[125] the younger brother of the master (Sananda Lal Ghosh), vividly describes what he saw when he went to his brother's room one night, (out of curiosity), to observe him in the deathless trance.

Sitting on the floor, facing his brother as he sat in the meditative posture on his bed, Sananda intently listened to "Mejda" sing a devotional song. After which he immediately became as lifeless as a statue! Observing this for over an hour, Sananda became quite alarmed, as there was no response after calling his brother's name several times. Neither could

---

125   Los Angeles, California: Self-realization Fellowship, 1980. (Mejda means second eldest brother, in Bengali).

he get a response by shaking him quite vigorously. And he became even more alarmed, when after checking, he realized neither was his brother breathing, nor did he have a heartbeat.

The witness to this metaphysical state was also "Mejda's" father, who came in search of Sananda, who was supposed to be sleeping in his room. And it was not until his father applied some yogic techniques, did "Mejda" return to full consciousness a couple hours later!

As is expected, a disciple's incredible feats can easily be emulated by their master. And this case involves (Yogananada); seeing his guru – Sri Yukteswar, in the deathless state.

While spending one of his occasional nights at his master's ashram,[126] it was unusual for Yogananda not to get the customary instructions from his guru to put down the mosquito nets before they slept. And that night it needed to be done quite soon, as the critters were out in force and attacking as though they hadn't tasted blood in some time. Getting up from his cot, after failing to catch his master's attention with a cough or two, Yogananda approached his master's bed nearby and was shocked to find he was as still as a corpse and he wasn't breathing. What Yogananda did next evokes a trace of hilarity, as to make sure his master was still among the living the panicked disciple first held a mirror to his nose – for traces of vapour. Then he forcibly held-shut his nose and mouth simultaneously for several minutes. Both "tests" which gave the dire indication that the master was dead. As Yogananda was hurrying to the door to get help, the amused master came out of his yogic trance just in time to prevent the sounding of a false alarm.[127]

Although this third case is not a narrative of an objective experience, it is nonetheless an attestation to the reality of this divine state.

---

126 Located in Serampore, (a resort town in West Bengal, India).

127 Recounted in *Autobiography of a Yogi*, page 126.

The great master, Sri Chinmoy, who has accomplished more in one lifetime,[128] than most of us in many, gave this response to his disciple when he was asked why she felt her heart stop, during her meditations.

In her case, he said, "It was an experience of her physical being, surrendering to the Divine, within." But more importantly he went on to state that this was a state quite common to the great yogis, and that in fact, he himself first accomplished this in his early teens, at his ashram in India, and subsequently went on to do so (entering the deathless state), on several other occasions.[129]

THE AURA REVEALS OUR INNER DIVINITY

Our auras, which envelop our bodies with their wonderful display of fluctuating and vibrating colours, as with revealing our true nature at a physical level,[130] also give a true indication, of our level of spiritual evolution. As the more innate divinity we have awakened, the more golden-yellow our auras become. And unlike the average aura which only extends from the body for several feet. There is no limit to this golden-yellow aura, found around, God-realized men.

In her book: *Only God: A Biography of Yogi Ramsuratkumar*,[131] the seasoned writer Regina Ryan describes what an eleven-year-old clairvoyant girl saw, when she accompanied her parent to see the yogi at his ashram, in India. Unlike anything she had seen before, in observing the auras of those around her, she was utterly amazed to find the aura of the master extended as far as her eyes could see – in other words – it was limitless.

---

128 Apart from peace meditations, which he conducted twice weekly at the United Nations Headquarters in New York, Sri Chinmoy has written over 1,000 books; composed an untold number of devotional songs; and painted thousands of mystical paintings, which have been showcased at art galleries, throughout the world.

129 Excerpt from *Meditation: Man-Perfection in God-Satisfaction* by Sri Chinmoy. Jamaica, New York: Agni Press, 1978; page 268.

130 Reading auras is a science in itself. Once versed in it, one can easily tell if another is lying, in love, happy or sad, successful or a failure. In fact, it betrays every thought. But of far greater importance, illnesses show up in the aura; some while before they actually become manifest in our physical bodies, as uncharacteristic colorations, over the soon-to-be-affected areas.

131 Page 314. Prescott, Arizona: Hohm Press, 2004.

It was the same experience she'd had a little earlier when she visited Prasanthi Nilayam, the ashram of Sri Sathya Sai Baba (recognized by millions to be an avatar), where she observed the Holy Man's aura extending from horizon to horizon!

DIVINE POWER EXHIBITED

Unlike many illumined sages, who usually spend their lives in isolation, this renowned swami – who lived in the city of Banares, India, decades ago, displayed his wonders on an every-day basis – for all eyes to see!

Trailanga Swami could be seen floating on the holy waters of the Ganges for days at end, and other times he could be seen totally submerged beneath the waves, where he would remain for long periods of time.

He is known to have drunk poison on several occasions. And was even supposedly tricked into drinking a large bucket of calcium lime – used for white-washing walls; offered as being clabbered milk – by a skeptic, who wanted to expose him as being a charlatan. But instead of harming the swami, the poison had the opposite effect, with all the deadly symptoms being transferred to the evil-doer. Fortunately the compassionate swami, feeling the offender had learned his lesson, healed him!

Well known not to have a fancy for apparel (for one who is God-realized has lost all identification with the body), the master no doubt proved to be quite a handful for the law. He was imprisoned on several occasions by the local officers. And each time his three-hundred pound body (although he rarely ate), could be seen casually sitting on the prison roof. Despite their best efforts to keep him locked up; even having a guard in front of his cell – the outcome was always the comical same! He could be seen sitting atop the jail, in nothing more than his birthday suit.[132]

A searcher seeking the jewel of self-realization, having heard of the presence of the great Babaji, in the nearby mountains,[133] kept up his

---

132   The swami's episodes taken from: *Autobiography of a Yogi*; pages 316-318.
133   The master and his close disciples rarely stayed at one place for extended periods of time, but often settled in the Badrinarayan area, in northern India.

intense search for the master for several months, with no luck. Until he made his way up a challenging cliff and came upon a clearing, where he saw seated a personage, he believed to be him, surrounded by his close circle of disciples.

Approaching, the stranger said, "You must be the great Babaji," then beseechingly added, "Will you accept me as your disciple? Life would be meaningless without you to guide me to the Divine."

To which the master replied, "In your present state, you are not ready to be my disciple."

Feeling fully rejected at what he heard, the stranger said, "If you don't accept me, I will jump off this cliff."

"Do as you please," came the reply.

And without hesitation, the dejected man hurled himself, over the cliff!

The unemotional Babaji then sent his disciples to retrieve the mangled body of the lifeless man. Standing over it, he waved his divine hand, upon which the deceased now stood before him in living flesh, without a trace of harm. Then Babaji said, "You are now ready to become one of us; death will not touch you again!"[134]

Apart from his artistic accomplishments, which are in themselves incredible, what Sri Chinmoy accomplished in the physical arena, for someone not displaying any outward appearance of unusual physical strength, can only be classified as nothing short of being supernormal.

At an awards program he named, "Lifting up the world with a oneness of heart," he performed the Herculean feat of lifting several people – weighing over seventeen hundred pounds, on a specially constructed platform. A feat which should not be misconstrued as involving trickery, as he once even lifted, over seven thousand pounds![135]

134 From *Autobiography of a Yogi*, page 336.
135 Recorded in: *Death and Reincarnation: Eternity's Voyage* by Sri Chinmoy. Jamaica, New York: Aum Publications, 1997. Pages 139 and 140.

CONQUERING DEATH

Conquering death indeed sounds quite paradoxical. But it simply means victory or mastery over it – opening up the door to the "other side," when it's time to leave, and doing so effortlessly and gracefully. Nevertheless, being something we are not usually accustomed to hearing – it does sound foreign.

Although the concept is well known to those who practice a scientific spiritual technique, to gain self-realization. Albeit, it is known by the Sanskrit term – mahasamadhi.[136]

Something that is not so farfetched as it may seem, for there are many who practice astral projection – travelling in the astral body of light – then returning to their regular bodies. Which entails the same principle, excepting that in mahasamadhi, there is no returning.

The purpose of this section is to demonstrate that those who have become self-realized, who intuitively know beforehand the appointed time for their departure from this illusory world, consciously leave their bodies. Dropping the overcoats of the flesh with as much ease as one may disrobe from a piece of clothing. Or in other words or another way of saying – instead of being unceremoniously kicked out of their bodies, these illumined beings make a voluntary, dignified exit!!!

In the world of self-realized mystics, numerous are known to have "departed" this way. But here are three well known cases of those who have "cheated" – the Grim Reaper!

If it weren't enough that he displayed two bodies[137] while in the flesh, Pranabananda, a self-realized sage who gained early retirement by giving the rather unusual explanation that he felt an overwhelming current moving up his spine[138] and spreading to other parts of his body, (making him unable to perform his duties), demonstrates to us that one who has

---

136 Mahasamadhi also involves the uniting of the individual soul with Infinite Spirit!

137 Detailed narrative in chapter three of *Autobiography of a Yogi*.

138 An actual sensation experienced by those in deep meditation, as the kundalini current moves up the spine.

fulfilled the purpose for which he was created (merging with the Divine) proves – death is nothing but a game in delusion!

For when it was time for him to "leave," he was sitting in the yogic lotus pose, before a very large crowd he had just fed and addressed. He simply told his close disciple next to him that he would kick the bucket, and then turning his inner gaze to the divine eye in the forehead – he made his earthly exit!

It is a maxim among the masters that only one who has realized God can lead you to Him. From this perspective then, it should come as no surprise that when the time came for Pranabananda's guru, Lahiri Mahashaya, to leave the world of manifestation, he did it in like manner.

Sitting in his parlour, surrounded by his close disciples. The master taught from the Gita for many hours. Then simply uttered: "I am going home." He stood up, made three complete rotations, sat in the lotus position, facing north,[139] and ushered into the infinite!

In this third instance, Paramahansa Yogananda – whose guru SriYuk-teswar, was himself a disciple of Sri Mahashaya, also made a dramatic exit, from his body.

Speaking about God and India at a banquet in honour of a dignitary from his homeland. He concluded with a poem very close to his heart, and upon uttering the last word, his body slumped to the floor, exiting the world the way the masters do; that is – consciously.

A MIRACLE FROM THE OTHER SIDE

The popular sixteenth-century mystic – Kabir, who is also associated with the line of masters already mentioned, as he was initiated into the scientific God-realization technique – Kriya yoga by the deathless Babaji, displayed an even more dramatic twist when giving up his bodily temple.

At the time of his passing, there arose a great controversy amongst his disciples (who were both Muslims and Hindus), over whether his body

---

139 A Vedic rite, performed before entering mahasamadhi.

should be interred (traditional to the former), or cremated, (customary to the latter).

Settling the matter from beyond the grave by appearing before them, he said, "Now there should be no more discontent; each party take half of my remains and perform the rites according to your tradition." When the stunned devotees removed the shroud covering his body. Instead of the master, they found a bouquet of beautiful flowers!

THE GREAT BELIEF

In giving ourselves a chance to believe the above cases could be true. It could help us unequivocally to unravel the tangled threads of our false mortality. For if all men are created equal, yet some have risen to accomplish superhuman feats, which can only be considered as divine. Doesn't it stand to reason that men will only live as mortals until they're so desirous of re-claiming their God status?

BEYOND THE REALM OF THE NORM

Made in the image
Of Him that ruleth the universe
It's a downright absurdity
To think that that power,
Beyond the realm of the norm,
Exhibited by a brother human,
Can be viewed merely
As a power bestowed
Upon a select few,
When all are made equal!
The secret being:
They are the ones,
Who strived ardently and continuously
To find the key,
To unlock the mystical door,
To their latent, inherent Divinity!

CHAPTER 12 | Two Sides of The Coin

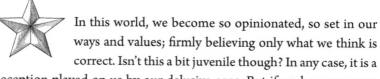 In this world, we become so opinionated, so set in our ways and values; firmly believing only what we think is correct. Isn't this a bit juvenile though? In any case, it is a deception played on us by our delusive egos. But if we become more open-minded, then we can look at both sides of the coin, and make a judgement that's much more logical – allowing us to grow in understanding and wisdom. And this is what, this chapter is all about!

It makes a lot of sense though: for if an apple and an orange were placed in front of some of the most intellectually qualified people on the planet. And ask them to taste only the apple. Then to tell you which fruit is sweeter. It is absolutely certain, as we all know, that they will all respond that: "That is an utterly stupid question. As one must first sample the orange too in order to give a true answer."

Yet, when we view other spiritual beliefs, different from our own, (which in most cases we adopted because of our family tradition); we immediately become biased towards them, to the extent that numerous wars were, and still being unnecessarily fought in this cause! touting our personal faith to be the only true religion; the one that will lead us to "paradise," and qualify us to sit on the right hand side of our Creator.

Although we don't even make the most basic attempt to study, analyze and try to understand what the essence of their teachings represent.

Something that became part of us, not too dissimilar to how we acquired a special taste for our traditional ethnic foods; or for the sports-minded who had no other alternative but to be involved in those professional sports, that were part of the mainstream, in their geographical location. Choices adopted not necessarily because they were the ideal, but rather chosen because of where we were destined to be born!

This one-sided view of the coin, also results in the misunderstandings that exist between ourselves, and others who are not of the same skin colour.

If we were to do a little deep thinking, as well as just an iota of anthropological research; it would become clear that the colour of our skin (hereditably obtained) is simply a feature of a race, given by God in accordance with the climatic conditions in the geographical location, where they were born. Darker colour given to certain races, to help them to be protected from the harsh rays of the sun, rather than a physical characteristic indicating that they are of a superior status.

It might be surprising to many that in the extreme north of India – the Kashmiri region because of its proximity to the snow-capped Himalayas; the people have very fair skin, blond hair and blue eyes; in distinct contrast to those living at the opposite end of the country, where it is intolerably hot.

The familiar adage: colour is skin deep, is more than aptly appropriate.

For in reality the body is simply an overcoat for the immutable, eternal and divine soul! – the individual spark – of the one Universal Flame. Hence this misunderstanding simply shows a clear lack of wisdom, in believing a man's colour makes him different from another, born of a different race.[140]

---

140 "God hath made of one blood all nations of men" (Acts 17:26).

This bias is also a great error in judgement. For in our countless births on our journey to "perfection," we ourselves have been clothed some time or the other, in a skin colour different from the one we currently "wear."[141]

But of more relevance: is the fact that according to the ironclad law of karma: the races for which one holds a strong negative disposition, will be the ones, he has to be rid of his prejudice, by being born as a member of that race. For being sons of the one Father, that bias will have to be karmically resolved, before the wave can make progress on its journey – to becoming one with the Ocean.

In like manner, any injustices inflicted on someone of another religious persuasion will have to be repaid according to the infallible law of karma.

The way we easily jump to hasty and inappropriate conclusions brings to mind a subtly humorous conversation that took place between the master, Sri Yogananda, and a broker friend of his, many years ago. During their lively discussion about saints and holy men in India, his friend indignantly voiced his opinion by saying that, "There are no true saints in India – they all lack spiritual realization."

In casually changing the topic, the master then went on to discuss brokers in Calcutta. And after intently listening to his friend express his thoughts on the subject. He interjected with saying, "It is hard to find an honest broker in Calcutta."

At which the broker flew into a fiery rage and rudely responded, "What do you know about brokers?"

Then Yogananda wittingly replied, "I don't know about brokers, what do you know about saints?" His friend being stumped, and having no reply, the yogi continued, "The only reason I said that was to show you how unfair you were in your assessment of saints – a subject you obviously know nothing about!"

A narrative, no less, that teaches a life lesson about a common foible we are all so guilty of!

---

141   Many persons undergoing past life regressions, have recalled past lives – being of a different race, and also of a different gender.

HAVING OUR PRIORITIES MIXED UP

Interestingly enough, before we make choices in our lives regarding issues such as our health, food, financial matters, and family relationships – the researchers have to be definitive, before we actually believe what they are saying. Yet, when it comes to fully understanding the most important and relevant to us as human beings – spiritual truths; we do the converse, and show the least amount of interest or enthusiasm and dedicate, the least amount of time.

Can we truly say we've really made a definite effort to actually verify our beliefs, or to find out for ourselves, what exactly God is? Or what exactly is our relation to Him?

Is it any wonder that Lord Jesus declared, "The harvest truly is plenteous, but the labourers are few."[142]

SUBCONSCIOUS PROGRAMMING

It is plausible to accept as fact that our unquestioning acceptance of our traditional beliefs may have stemmed from an emotional factor or subconscious fear. For if we can imagine being born into a faith where our immediate family had strong religious beliefs. And from the time our minds could form impressions, these teachings were impressed upon our consciousness. Then, as we grew a little older, and were exposed to the contents of our holy texts. Either through our own personal efforts, or from attending the house of worship related to our faith. These things, no doubt, will have had a very compelling influence; a form of subconscious programming that makes it hard to doubt that our religion is the only true path – that leads to blessings from above, and eternal salvation. And any deviation from it will have such dire consequences that the mere thought of trying to do so usually causes us to "tremble in fear!"

---

142   Matthew 9:37.

While in the same breath, it can genuinely be said that that those same teachings,[143] ironically invoke us to believe we are all sons of the one Father, who belong to the brotherhood of the human race!

So logic should dictate that it's not feasible to surmise that a Universal Heavenly Father would "send down" the quintessential spiritual teachings to one section of humanity, to the exclusion of others, when we are all equally created as his children – made in His image.

In the same way, it is a bit incredible to truly believe that as a consequence of adopting spiritual concepts different from our own, when we leave this earth we would have to endure the everlasting punishment of "hellfire." For, even for a human father to conceptualize this happening to an offspring of his, would prove absolutely unbearable. Much less so, for our Divine Father, to condemn us to this horrendous fate in the afterlife. This makes even much more sense when we consider that another name for the Divine – is Unconditional Love.

It would do us well to reconsider our religious biases, when we can learn to see that each religion had to be representative of the people born at a specified time,[144] and a specific place. In other words, it had to be presented in accordance to their level of consciousness by the "divine messenger" imparting it to them. And is in no way indicative that we should consider one religion as being of greater importance, than another.

If we were to give it some thought; New Age spiritual concepts that have become readily accessible and quite acceptable to so many of us. To even have considered a very small fraction of this information a few centuries back would have cost us our lives, because we would have been thought to be in cahoots with the "dark forces." And even not that far back (as already pointed out), just several decades ago, when *The Third*

---

143   Related to the great religions of the world.

144   Usually when they are sorely in need of spiritual hope and regeneration. "Whenever and wherever there is a decline in religious practice, and a predominant rise of irreligion – at that time I descend Myself to deliver the pious and to annihilate the miscreants, as well as to reestablish the principles of religion, I Myself appear, millennium after millennium' (Bhagavad Gita IV:7 and 8). Verse seven also quoted in chapter 10.

Eye, came out, it became a "hard sell" with the public and now with an unusually high number of printings has gone on to become – a metaphysical masterpiece!

TRUE FAITH REQUIRES TRUE DEVOTION

A not-too-perfect situation that arises even in our own traditional belief system is that we don't take our teaching literally and rationalize it to suit our purposes. The following story being also funny – clearly depicts this.

There is a certain religionist (an acquaintance of mine), whose faith absolutely forbids the imbibing of intoxicating beverages and playing games of chance. So apart from being a teetotaler, this personage adamantly refuses to partake of baked products (such as cakes), which constitute alcohol as an ingredient, although having a sweet tooth and being exceptionally fond of them. Yet, he gets out of bed before the crack of dawn and heads down to the casino (a good distance away), so he can participate in high-stakes poker tournaments.

Rather realistically, is it any wonder that Christ uttered these universal words of wisdom: "And why call ye me, Lord, Lord, and do not the things which I say?"[145]

It would be rather alarming if we were able to get a figure to see how many of us claiming to be true religionists are truly guilty of this type of transgression.

If we are able to reflect and scrutinize at a higher level, we would also be able to see, more often than not, that the practice of our faith is more of an attraction to the outer forms of religion, rather than genuinely and resolutely trying to make a deeper connection with the Divine.

We'll find although being unflinchingly allegiant toward our faith. We're more seriously concerned about such exteriorizations like; the size and appearance of our "place of worship"; the status of the people who attend it; the level of exhilarating emotion stirred up within us (which, by the

---

145   Luke 6:46

way, quickly subsides as soon as we're out of the doors of the institution) by the captivating oratory[146] of the leader of the congregation; or being over-pleased that one is attending a place of worship that has numerous attendees. Instead of when leaving a prayer gathering, we can genuinely say we've made some permanent progress on our journey to the Divine!

This is not the way it was meant to be, though, because all great religions provide guidelines, laid down to bring our latent and innate sattvic (spiritual) qualities to the fore. That is religious observances such as – moral and spiritual codes. And it's because we've played down this part of our spiritual teaching – that we are catering more to the whims of the stimulation of our senses – rather than to the awakening of our true spiritual nature – that purifies our hearts and creates genuine devotion and allows us to be more in tune with our Creator.

INTUITION REVEALS TRUTH

The greatest secret of religion is not to stoop to the contemptible level of bickering and fighting about whose religion is better and greater. (A misleading attitude that prevents us from significantly progressing from our materially-bound condition). In fact, even if we were to change our spiritual customs, or if there was a unification of all forms into one common belief system, this would still not bring about an enormous change in our spiritual attitude or spiritual realization, for until the latter is fully attained (through striving manfully to – repossess our divine heritage), there still will be the practice of religion on a "part-time" basis. For what matters most is the depth of our thirst for self-realization, along with purity of heart, and not from which spiritual well we choose to imbibe from. But at the same time, we have to soundly realize our minds have to be tended by ourselves, our efforts our own, spiritual truths will not magically fall into our laps. On attaining this God-realized state, (alas, however, a feat fast lacking in a world where sheer materialism acts as

---

146 Excellent oratory does not necessarily depict spiritual realization, but oft-times is just a natural gift of expressing any form of knowledge.

more than a convenient substitution for true spiritualism), the traits of passion and ignorance are effortlessly discarded into the background; all doubts who we truly are and the underlying unity of all religions are intuitively revealed. Hence the ignorance of bias towards other spiritual beliefs is finally dissolved – being burnt in the self-realization of truth!

Or even if we were just to ponder this remarkable point; if different religions were meant to create biases, disharmony, and distrust, then the sacred command taught by the great religions (although each has it worded in a different way); Love thy neighbor as thy self, would be an extremely self-contradictory – pronouncement. And if we can justifiably agree with this, then it should be easy to see there is only one religion – the religion of love, and only one God – and He is the Universal Father!

Upon grasping these great truths, man automatically adheres to the divine laws (commandments) that instruct him to feel brotherly love for all, and to love God with all his heart, soul, might, and strength. And in doing so complying willingly and easily to the Lord's other scriptural commands becomes second nature.[147] Consequently, his prayers become more focused, soulful, and sincere, hence making it much easier for all obstructive barriers between Creator and we, the created, to be dismantled. Which when accomplished boils down to fulfilling the sole purpose for which we were created; reuniting with the Divine Master of the universe!

A state which is sweetly and majestically put by the English mystical writer, of the seventeenth century – Thomas Traherne, in his spiritual classic *Centuries of Meditations*.[148] "You will never enjoy the world aright till the sea itself floweth in your veins, till you are clothed with the heavens, and crowned with the stars, and perceive yourself to be the sole heir of the whole world, and more than so, because men are in it who are everyone sole heirs as well as you."

---

147   A situation easily understood if we consider loving our earthly father with the same absolute passion.

148   London: Dobell, 1908.

THE PERSONAL AND IMPERSONAL GOD

All religions teach about the omnipresence of the Almighty. That is, the perpetual immanence of His presence in all creation, as well as beyond it. Along with the ability to do "as He pleases" – being omnipotent. From these doctrines, we can come to a great realization. For therefore then, He must be in us (as so often mentioned), as well as He can put a veil over His presence within us. The only problem being the majority of us are not only unaware of this, but included are some who think that this is an absolutely preposterous premise.

Now, as we know, different faiths offer their devotions to different aspects of the Divine. For example, some worship Rama, Krishna, Shiva, Buddha, Jesus, Shirdi Baba, Sathya Sai Baba, et al., while others deify the Unseen, Formless God! By the sheer force of numbers, the aggregate of those worshipping the Personal God, seems to be just as great, or maybe even greater in number than those who deify the Unseen Absolute. From this standpoint it seems logical to conclude that belief in a personal God is just as fundamental to human lives as the belief in the latter. And this realization is of great relevance to this volume. For all the aforementioned godheads, once "walked the earth" like you and me. And when through many incarnations they perfected themselves and attained oneness with the Transcendental Divine; no longer bound to the earth plane, being free from material desires and earthly attachments, they nevertheless "come down" to walk among us, and teach the way that shows – we can attain to their divine state, as well.

Added to this, a good question to ask ourselves is; if the Divine is eternally omnipresent, while at the same time being omnipotent – why can't he come in human form? and for that reason, why not in any form? (Is not the unseen substance steam, when condensed – becoming first water, and then ice – not the same product?") But by logic, we must understand, He has to come in a form that we can trust, be familiar and comfortable with. And importantly too, if we truly examine the lives of these avatars, we'll clearly see that although wearing the cloak of a human form, their earthly motives were in no way similar to ours. For they did not hanker after earthly possessions, nor did they try to control us, but rather were the epitome of unconditional love and selfless service.

Although at the same time – having full capabilities to perform miracles, of an unlimited nature!

In light of trying to show that despite all the outward differences and display of divisiveness, in essence, all religions propose the same truth, and also why we may have developed some of our religious biases, hopefully we'll realize that there should be no quarrel with other religions. But rather, if we could only endeavor instead, to put a little more steadfast and genuine effort in aspiring to attain what our faith is supposed to bring to the fore; namely the ultimate union of our soul with that of the Heavenly Father. Maybe, we'll be able to have a glimpse of the other side of the coin, without having to really flip it over!

TWO SIDES OF THE COIN

It's not uncommon to think
We're virtually right
Most of the time
Because of the very delusive ego!

It seems natural, when we think
Our point of view
Is all that matters,
Why take seriously, any other?

But in the "big picture"
Is this logical?
Is this realistic?
Is this laudable?
Think deeply and ponder!
It is quite unreasonable.

So keep an open mind,
Be receptive to other's opinions,
Always evaluate deeply,
"Two sides of the coin,"
And gain in understanding
Each and every time!

CHAPTER 13

Secrets of The Soul

 Maybe one of the most baffling questions in man's life, apart from some knowing that it is the spark of divinity within us, is where can he find some real informative material on the soul? And that is an extremely good question. Because it is very difficult to express something of an infinite nature with a finite mind.

It should be comforting then to know that all the information in this chapter is gleaned from different literary works by my guru – Paramahansa Yogananda, from information extracted from volumes authored by other God-realized masters. And from the voice of the Divine Himself – Lord Krishna; extracted from the Bhagavad Gita.

But where do we start, when dealing with such an absolutely profound subject? To get a better grasp, it would be prudent to start with an insight into some of the soul's inherent qualities.

A QUALITATIVE DEPICTION

This divine aspect of our being naturally being Cosmic Consciousness,[149] because of our limited, mortal condition can only be perceived as individual consciousness!

---

149   The presence of the Divine spread throughout creation, as well as beyond it.

A more exacting picture of its nature cannot be found than that depicted in the Gita: "The soul is unborn, eternal, ever-existing and primeval."[150] As a corollary; " The soul can never be cut to pieces by any weapon, nor burned by fire,[151] nor moistened by water, nor withered by the wind."[152] (An eye-opener indeed to man, who thinks by killing another, he is ridding himself of his grudges and anger. When in fact, he is just building on what he has to pay retribution for).

The soul is also immutable, illimitable, and omniscient. As well as possesses this other greatly fascinating aspect. (As like God, who created us and is in everything, and yet impartial.)[153] The soul is the detached beholder and silent witness to the transient scenes of pain and pleasure that play out on the screen, of our worldly consciousness.[154]

And to utilize a term used in ancient, sacred Indian texts, as well as by God-realized masters to describe the Creator. The soul is often referred to as satchitananda. That is ever-existing, ever-conscious, ever-new bliss.[155] (The last being the singular reason those who have realized truth show an utter disinterest in the world's fleeting joys!)

It is rather paradoxical indeed. We appear to be born, because of the birth of the material body. When in fact: our true nature is actually eternal.

---

150 II:20.

151 Which should further allow us to buy into the case: there is no hell.

152 II:23.

153 "...Although I am the maintainer of all living entities and although I am everywhere, I am not a part of this cosmic manifestation. All this work cannot bind Me, I am ever detached from all these material activities, seated as neutral" (Bhagavad Gita IX:5,9).

154 "Despite contact with the material body...the soul neither does anything nor is entangled" (Ibid XIII:32).

155 Although, almost impossible to put into words, it has been said by God-realized masters that the sum of all the glory, enjoyment, pleasure, and happiness of the world, could not even compare with a small fraction of this bliss of the soul!

THE SOUL AS LIGHT

And to get a more tangible feel for its nature, we have to take a look at what the Divine Himself has been depicted as.

First this quote immediately gets to the point. "God is light."[156] And as is commonly known to many of us. The Divine appeared as light (fire) on mount Sinai, when he delivered the Ten Commandments to the prophet Moses.[157]

But coming to a depiction in much more recent times: Sri Yogananda describes in his divine experience (not a singular one, but accessible to all who enter the blissful superconscious state of samadhi), in his state of God communion, what the Divine "looks like!"

He saw all creation as made of light.[158] Emanating from a divine, eternal source, a subtle radiance, which became more pronounced as it condensed into universes, planets, continents, trees, and beings, which simultaneously alternated from "matter" to a diaphanous unifying luster![159]

So just like this depiction of the Heavenly Father as light, inherently being Divine Intelligence, similarly the "son" (that's us) as the divine spark – the soul, can be seen to be made of the same essence.

However, a most extraordinary quality, difficult to be conceived by the human mind is that unlike any illumination in physical creation, it does not cast a shadow, neither does it radiate any heat.

---

156 1 John 1:5.
157 Exodus 24:15-17.
158 It is no coincidence then (as already stated in chapter seven) that everything is made up of energy. For as we all know – light is a form of energy!
159 Excerpt from *Autobiography of a Yogi*: pages 161 and 162.

THE SOUL AND THE PHYSICAL BODY

When the divine soul, encased in its two bodies – the astral[160] and causal,[161] comes into incarnation, it enters the united sperm and ovum at the time of conception.[162] Its intelligent life force then flows down the astral spine (sushumna) from its seat in the medulla, activating the creative powers of the lower chakras, which then go on to "build" the type of body it needs, to experience its current life's lessons in its evolution towards reunion with the Divine! Commencing with the medulla, the brain, and the spinal cord. Followed by the other body parts. It then settles in a coiled passage in the lowest chakra (muladhara, in the astral body). And because of where it comes to reside, this divine life energy is henceforth referred to as kundalini, from Sanskrit – kudala —meaning coiled.

With the "building" of the physical body completed, the three bodies are tied together and work as one, by a knotting of the life force from the astral body and consciousness from the causal body in the seven divine centers, or chakras.

The kundalini current now emanates outward from the coiled passage, making its entry into the physical body through the nerves. Where it gives life to the five senses of taste, touch, smell, sight, and hearing, and also

---

160 The astral body can become infinitely larger or smaller, as it so desires.

161 An ideational body of pure consciousness in which the soul first makes its entry. "It contains the thirty-five ideational principles; nineteen astral and sixteen physical, the soul requires for its interaction with God's creation. The nineteen ideas that make up the elements of the astral body are: "intelligence; ego; feeling; mind (sense consciousness); five instruments of knowledge (the subtle powers behind the physical sense organs); five instruments of action (the powers for the executive abilities to procreate, excrete, talk, walk and exercise manual skill); and five instruments of life force (those empowered to perform the crystallizing, assimilating, eliminating, metabolizing, and circulatory functions of the physical body). The physical body, unlike the astral body which is made up of mental, emotional, and lifetronic (pertaining to prana or life force) elements, is constituted of sixteen elements of a physical nature." See *Man's Eternal Quest* by Paramahansa Yogananda. Los Angeles, California: Self-Realization Fellowship, 1982. Pages 271 and 272.

162 A highly contentious subject indeed, but it is more realistic that the soul (life) is in the seed cell from the time of conception. For it is highly unlikely it could continue further development. Without this spark of life (the soul) being present, from the "inception!"

to the overwhelmingly earth-binding sex force, thereby enabling man (his consciousness) to identify and interact with the physical world.[163]

At the same time, the soul's life force and consciousness also enter the physical body through the brain and spine, and thence outward into the nervous system, organs, and senses. Like the life-giving sun that shines its light and sustains God's creation; the light of the soul pervades and sustains the entire physical body.

Because man's interaction through the senses with the material world becomes so strong, he becomes completely oblivious of being a divine being. And now believing himself to be solely a physical creation – the divine soul – "becomes" the delusive ego."[164]

With the last knotting of the three bodies taking place at the base of the spine – at the muladhara chakra – in which the "sleeping" kundalini is "housed," it becomes very difficult to retrace its steps into the heavenly astral kingdom.

To regain our inherent divine status, we must learn to open this knot of astral and physical power, so that the primal intelligent life force (kundalini) can ascend the path from which it came down, untethering the other knots and freeing the divine astral body from bondage to physical confinement. In this process, the chakras "awaken" and their "petals" turn upward, freeing the soul's attention from the material world, allowing our consciousness to soar from the world of matter to first expand into superconsciousness[165] at the medulla (connected by polarity to the ajna chakra), into Christ Consciousness[166] at the ajna chakra – and instead of just perceiving sensations from our immediate surroundings, we can now

---

163 Because the kundalini current is powerfully lured to the attractions of the material world and is deluded from not returning to its true home in the astral body – it is referred to: as being dormant.

164 "The senses are so strong and impetuous that they forcibly carry away the mind even of a man of discrimination who is endeavouring to control them" (Bhagavad Gita II:60).

165 The consciousness in which the world-conscious soul (the ego) realizes its true identity; being the divine light that "came down" from Eternal Spirit and not the bulb of the material flesh.

166 The projected consciousness of God in all creation.

"pick up" any "impulse" in the universe, as being part of our awareness;[167] then into Cosmic Consciousness at the thousand petaled lotus (sahasrara chakra), allowing us to become one again, with the Source from which we have become, so misleadingly separated!

SUBCONSCIOUS CONTACT WITH THE SOUL

If we were to give the state of sleep some serious thought, we would gain some unusually great insights as to whom we really are.

For if losing physical-body consciousness is the reality of death, wouldn't the corollary be that when we are restfully sleeping (a state in which the physical body is essentially lifeless), we should also be clinically dead. But quite the contrary is true, for as we all know, upon waking we can always recall the restless and agitating thoughts that prevented us from having a good night's sleep, or conversely, we can bring to mind the rejuvenating state we experienced, which allows us to feel like a "brand-new" person, upon awaking. Or, even in our state of slumber, oft-times we can be cognizant that we are not sleeping restfully, as our minds still keep "humming away!" So there must be something other than the body that remains conscious, when we are fast asleep.

In fact, a very remarkable thing occurs when we are asleep. The life force involuntarily withdraws from the muscles and sense telephones, and retires to the heart, spine, and brain areas[168] and we become aware, in a subconscious way (albeit only for a temporary time), of our inherent, divine nature. Isn't it amazing? We temporarily forget all about the body and its associations. We no longer identify ourselves as being of a specific nationality, nor do we remember our gender, or who our beloved family

---

167 If we could only but realize that our minds are capable of illimitable expansion. Then this super-human feat should not be too difficult to fathom. For the corollary would be that the consciousness that resides in it must possess the same capability too!

168 What occurs here is consciously reproduced by yogis, who use scientific methods of meditation to withdraw the life force and consciousness, and thus can consciously experience their divine soul nature, and through steadfast effort and blessings from their God-realized gurus, can eventually go on to merge with: Infinite Spirit!

is, nor do we feel any attachment to our earthly possessions. But we are so deluded by the material world and its attractions – that as soon as we open our eyes, our egos "kick in" and we believe ourselves to be the body. And we lose that temporary, delightful identification, with our true selves!

(Interestingly enough, in much the same way as the projection of moving pictures requires electrical energy and film before they can be "played out," in like manner, we use this same withdrawn life force (energy), plus subconscious memories, thoughts, and reactions of the subtle senses,[169] to create the fascinating "movies of the mind.")

Another revealing piece of evidence that sheds light on the delusionary nature of the body, occurs during our dreams. For when we are dreaming, we are able to have sentient experiences through the subconscious mind just as if we were awake – having them through the conscious mind. For example, we have all had experiences where we are partaking of delicious dishes and refreshing beverages—although our actual physical sense of taste is inactive – or enjoying beautiful scenery, or being absorbed in listening to some type of music or the other (although our eyes are closed, and the physical sense of hearing is nonfunctional too). And we all know these experiences are not taking place through our physical sense organs. Is it not? And this is because, although they belong to the physical body, sensory perception itself is actually a function of man's astral body of subtle electricities.[170] And allows us to have normal sentient experiences during sleep, although the entire physical body, for all intents and purposes, is quite "lifeless."

---

169 Explained in the next paragraph.

170 A fact already mentioned in this chapter under the footnotes – of the ideational body. Which indicate that the physical senses are actually a function of the five instruments of knowledge, which constitute five of the nineteen elements found in the astral body.

THE SOURCE OF INTUITION IS THE SOUL

As we all know, when we perceive things through the five senses there is usually great room for error, for depending on our frames of mind at different times, the information fed to us through the intellect isn't always correct. Or, worded another way, interpretations by the mind of sensory stimuli are oft-times erroneous. And this is because the intellect gives us only a partial, or indirect, view of things. Whereas, intuition is an absolute grasping of truth; that is seeing it by being one with it! No surprise then why intuition is known as the sixth sense, because the grasp of information we derive from it is entirely independent of our physical senses.

But more importantly, the reason why things we intuitively feel happen to be totally correct is because they are a direct feeding of information from the all-knowing, divine soul, as opposed to the inferential data fed to us – from the continually thought-creating, worldly mind. If then, we are certain the information we receive (usually we can differentiate it, as being distinct from our regular thoughts) is from this sixth sense. We should always pay heed to it. For being a divine source, it cannot possibly be wrong.

Unfortunately, in as much as this sixth sense is inherent in all. Because of skepticism, compounded with the fact that the "receiving station" varies from person to person, owing to the difference in calmness of minds; many do not share in this wonderful, "spiritual experience!"

A PARALLELISM

We would be able to garner great hope and solace if we were to think deeply about the following parallelism. A royal personage, losing his way in the slums and then becoming inebriated, does not forfeit his royal status. As soon as he sobers up, and painstakingly finds his way home, he is royalty again. And so we too, getting lost in the labyrinths of the material world, and becoming "mentally distorted" with its earthly attractions and our attachments, do not really lose our spiritual "royal" status. It is always there for the reclaiming if we were to approach the goal (the divine kingdom) upon our "reawakening" with intense fervor. But make no mistake (as pointed out before), to regain such a lofty position doesn't come easily – it will not be deposited in our laps.

THE MUSK DEER

This narrative about the musk deer also proves to be an illuminating piece of information. The musk deer is highly prized for an extract located in a sac under the skin of the abdomen, from which the quite popular fragrances are prepared. As the deer reaches a certain age, the highly aromatic substance oozes out of its navel. Confounded as to the source of this overpowering smell, they run hither and thither in a vain effort to locate it. Finding their search utterly fruitless, many of them become wildly insane and hurl themselves off the high mountain-tops upon which they live. Without ever realizing what they so desperately seek is right under their skin.

Like the deer, man is also forever looking for something; that elusive, unmistakable something that will bring him complete and permanent happiness and contentment. But despite his countless material accomplishments and attachments, he still cannot pinpoint its source. Because he does not realize his eternal quest will not end until he turns his focus inwards – allowing him to reconnect with his "long-lost" divine soul. If not, time will prove he will have to face (because we live in a world of duality, as well as having a lot of karma to repay) many unavoidable, painful experiences, if the searchlight of his attention continues to focus outwards.

NO FEAR OF DEATH

And lastly, we should have no fear of death, for we subconsciously experience it every night when we go to sleep. (The conscious mind ceases to exist, just as in death – does it not?) The only really major difference being that in the "big sleep" there will be no more association with a physical body – well, at least not until our next incarnation. Also, in our evolutionary process, we have experienced it many more times than we would care to imagine!

Here is an extremely relevant Biblical quote, (timeless words from Lord Jesus):

> "The Father [the God-realized soul]
> That dwelleth in me,
> He doeth the works [miracles] . . .
> I am in the Father
> And the Father in me!"[171]

---

171 John 14:10, 11 (verse 11 also used in chapter seven).

| CHAPTER 14 | The Divine Sound |

 Here is a mystical word that has crossed the path no doubt, like the third eye of many, many a man but alas – only a few really know its true meaning. They may have a vague notion that it is connected to yoga, meditation, certain mantras, and various prayers of an Eastern nature. And of course, readers of this volume would have had a brief and oblique introduction to it, from chapter seven. But make no mistake, a realization of its true meaning can be no less than a wonderful blessing, in disguise!

This arcane, oft misconstrued, divine word is Aum or Om, and is unmistakably as old as time itself. For it is the sound made by the intelligent, all-creative, vibratory force that "came forth" from the "bosom" of the Divine that structures, maintains, and guides the universe according to the divine plan. Or more simply described; it is the sound of the vibratory, creative, or cosmic energy that "went out" of God to manifest the universe. And hence as also mentioned in chapter seven, everything in the phenomenal world, characterized by the world of opposites, possesses this inherent quality of vibration.

Yet this whir of the cosmic motor is mysteriously obscured from our mortal hearing, which for all intents and purposes is just too poor a faculty (like the other senses, whose failings have also been pointed out previously), to perceive things of the Spirit! "They seeing see not; and hearing they hear not, neither do they understand."[172]

Apart from being the most sacred syllable in the most ancient of the scriptural texts – the Vedas. It is alluded to, as being comprised of the supreme combination of letters.[173] It's no coincidence then that even the individual letters have deep symbolic significance: A stands for akara, or the creative vibration; U for ukara, the preservative vibration; and M for makara, the vibratory power of dissolution[174] – the three stages of all creations in the material world.

And now this enlightening revelation of a little-known scriptural fact. This divine word became the sacred Hum of the Tibetans; Amin of the Moslems; and Amen of the Egyptians, Greeks, Romans, Jews and Christians.[175] (And for the curious, this oft-used sacred word – Amen, means sure or faithful in Hebrew).

With the emanation of this vibratory force from beyond creation, came into being naturally too, the defining standards of this realm of transient existence; the three dimensions of space and the fourth dimension of time. (And of course the basic building blocks of all creation – the atom, in which the much more microscopic particles, the electrons display their incessant vibrations, exemplifying the vibratory nature of creation.)

In this human drama, these standards of the phenomenal world are not what they seem to be. With time, we are accustomed to seeing all events and situations as being in the past, present, or the future. When in fact everything is occurring in the current moment, having no essence of ambiguity. For as most of us are aware, past and future are simply reference points, created in the "recesses of our minds." The reality being that in the realm of ever-conscious, ever-Eternal Spirit, there is no concept of time; only – the "eternal now!"

---

172   Matt. 13:13 (one may recall this quote also used in chapter one).
173   Bhagavad Gita VIII:13.
174   Excerpt from *The Yoga of Christ*, page 27
175   See *The Divine Romance*, page 464.

Similarly, with space, this erroneously gives the illusory impression of limitless divisions. When in fact there is no space, for all forces can start at one point or expand everywhere. However, the divine ruse being the relativities of creation, space and time present the idea of change and division to perpetuate the continual illusion of the material world being real! (And it will remain so, until our consciousness expands beyond the current range of our limited senses!)

CREATION'S ORIGIN

All major religions proclaim the Mighty Hand of the Divine as the source of all creation. Is it not? Or if viewed from another angle, since they also proclaim, "We are made in His image." And since we are in creation, of the greatest importance, it stands to reason all the secondary things that provide us with the necessities of life must be created by His divine hands, too! So the material here not only corroborates this but does much more. It lets the cat out of the bag as to the rather ingenious and utterly enigmatic means employed by the Mighty Hand of the Divine, to bring the cosmos into manifestation.

In this context then, the Indivisible (the Divine) appears divided, through the delusive process by which He differentiates Himself into multifarious creations through their different rates of vibration. In essence, the only definitive identifying characteristic that makes as diverse "items" as thoughts, consciousness, X-rays, solids, liquids, gases etc., appear different, is their rate of vibration! As opposed to His divine state before creation, in which the state of being, the act of perception, and the object of perception are all One; hence there is no vibration.

AUM'S INHERENT INTELLIGENCE

As already mentioned, the Cosmic Motor possesses intelligence. And what does all this mean? Well! Off hand, we know it would be rather impractical and utterly chaotic if it were left "unattended." Just imagine a started vehicle, minus a driver, allowed to "cruise" down the highway!

So the Divine imbued His cosmic vibration with His Infinite Intelligence, which when manifested into planets, universes, plants, animals, and human life is called Christ Consciousness. Many may recall the indigo-blue sphere within the celestial eye is a representation of this. As well as the golden halo, being representative of the universal cosmic vibration.

Like the noble title Buddha, which was bestowed upon the prince, Gautama, Christ is also an honorific title bestowed on the divine Jesus, to signify he had become like the Buddha; one with the Christ Consciousness. A perennially unfulfilled goal, which all of us must one day attain!

BOSE'S EXPERIMENTS

To get a better understanding of this, we'll look at the incredibly fascinating work done by the scientist, Dr. J. C. Bose, over a hundred years ago, for which he received the Nobel Prize.

He demonstrated, using his marvelous scientific apparatus of his own creation, and with an exceedingly high magnification, that both plants and seemingly inanimate substances such as metals, inherently possess some type of very sensate awareness, as they respond to stimuli in much the same way as we do.

When chloroform was applied to a plant and a sample of tin, they appeared anything but inert, displaying constant, slow motions[176] on a screen. The amazing pantomime suddenly came to a halt. And the silent movie show immediately resumed, when an antidote was applied to the former. After a period of recuperation had elapsed, the tin became "alive," too!

The more drastic measure of severing the stem of the plant, produced the state of permanent stillness characteristic with death.

The same outcome resulted when a poisonous chemical was applied to the seemingly lifeless sample of metal.

---

176   The motions from the plant (a fern) were due to being in a continuous state of growth, while those from the sample of tin were caused by the vibrations of the microscopic structural particles – the atoms.

Although listing only a few of the experiments, the picture intended to be painted, was accomplished. Revealing, the Christ Consciousness principle isn't that far-fetched, after all!

SCRIPTURAL REFERENCES

And now for some scriptural references, alluding to this divine sound, not only from the Bible, but also from the seemingly contrasting Eastern scriptures. Similarities that support the point that generally conceived divisions are not really what they seem.

"In the beginning was the Word, and the Word was with God, and the Word was God. All these things were made by Him, and without Him was not any thing made that was made."[177]

To break this down; "beginning" refers to the birth of creation. For Eternal Absolute Spirit has no beginning, for It is ever-conscious, ever-existing. "Word" signifies sound energy or vibration, originating from a source of intelligent thinking or thought, (which is the divine sound – Aum, imbued with Christ Consciousness). It is just as if we were to utter the word "love"; it would naturally have to be the result of the direct use of thought, indicating intelligence. Is it not? As well as it would evidently have to possess sound energy, or be vibrational in nature. "And the Word was with God," refers to the "Word" (the Aum vibration imbued with the omnipresent Christ Consciousness), being part of Him, before being sent forth into creation. "And the Word was God" means there is no difference or separate identity between the "Word" (Aum vibration) and God.

There is no need to explain the second part of the quote, as it is self-evident. In any event, here is another quote to reinforce the point about the way it was – in the beginning! "These things saith the Amen [the Word, Aum], the faithful and true witness, the beginning of the creation of God."[178]

---

177   John 1:1, 3.
178   Rev. 3:14.

In bringing forth creation – it means it could not be different from Himself. For a creation by the Absolute cannot be anything but the same. But two ever-existing infinite forces cannot co-exist. There can be only one! It is common knowledge that in creating something, there will always be the distinction between the creator and the created. So in making a differentiation between Himself and His creation, He created the delusive veil of maya (a Sanskrit word meaning: the Measurer), to camouflage the omnipresence of Spirit hidden beneath this manifestation. Wherein everything that is manifested in the phenomenal world, appears to be limited, divisive, and without exception – dualistic. (How can there not be evil forces, when there has to be the opposite of good?) In much the same way a tranquil ocean becomes distorted into multifarious waves by the disrupting activity of a turbulent storm.

In bringing forth creation, also, the Uncreated, Unmanifested Spirit became the trilogy. That is God the Father – the Transcendent Absolute beyond creation; God the Son – His omnipresent presence in creation, as Christ consciousness; and the Holy Ghost – the cosmic vibration – Aum, which structures and upholds all creation.

In describing the genesis of creation, the hoary Vedas state, Vak – the cosmic vibratory Word was with Prajapati the Divine, in the beginning of creation, and by Vak – the intelligent vibration that emanated from Him, all things that were "made," were made. And Vak and Prajapati are one.

They also refer to God, the Father, as Sat; God the Son as Tat;[179] and the Holy Ghost as Aum; (the latter being obvious, as that's where the cosmic syllable, was first recorded). And the omniscient divine Christ Consciousness "within" the Aum vibration is referred to as: Kutastha Chaitanya.

---

179 Sat and Tat, one may recall being referred to in chapter seven, also

PRACTICAL VERIFICATION

These scriptural references should not be taken as merely theory or theological concepts, for anyone knowing the correct scientific meditational techniques, as taught by a self-realized master, can, after steadfast effort and commitment, be able to hear for himself this divine sound emanating from every particle of creation. And in so doing, would be actually listening, literally, to the "voice of God." An experience that echoes the one already mentioned, whereby those with their celestial eye opened, hear the sound like the mighty roar of the ocean – (the Aum vibration) – the culmination of all the sounds made by the lower five chakras.

By repeated practice of listening to this Aum sound, (expression of the cause of creation), which is omnipresent, one's consciousness becomes the same; or in other words, one's mortal consciousness expands to infinity. One's tiny soul wave merging once again, with the Ocean of Spirit! Man to God. Is it not?

In his Gospel, St. John exhorts us to pay heed to this wonderful teaching from his master: "But as many as received him, to them gave he power to become the sons of God, even to them that believe on his name."[180] A reference to those hearing the Aum vibration, becoming in tune with its inherent Christ Consciousness (from which the "Master" got his honorific title), attaining oneness with the Father as he had done. Thus the words: "become the sons of God." Continuing with the rest of the quote: "Which were born, not of blood, nor of the will of the flesh, nor of the will of man, but of God."[181] Obviously, becoming "the sons of God" – has nothing to do with the flesh! But of a bloodline in Spirit!

180 John 1:12.
181 John 1:13.

SCIENTIFIC VIEWPOINT

It's no secret that for decades before his passing, the great physicist, Albert Einstein, was working on the so-called unified field theory – a theory postulating a common "thread," unifying the fabric of all nature's forces. However, let's say the "revelatory vibrations" in the ether were not as friendly to him, it not being the right time in the current Yuga.

Nevertheless, there is no doubt he was evidently on the right track. For with the dawn of the twenty-first century, scientists are on the cusp of proving the theory a reality. Prior to this, it was determined that the most fundamental particles of which the physical universe is comprised are; electrons, quarks – the building blocks of protons and neutrons (particles "inhabiting" the nucleus of an atom), and neutrinos. Although, in essence, they are uniquely different. For example, electrons have a negative charge, while neutrinos have no charge, at all.

But string theory may be lifting the veil about the mystery of creation by declaring at the ultramicroscopic level there is only one fundamental particle – the string. Stemming from a single source as it vibrates, it brings into manifestation a specific object. The only criterion differentiating any two "creations" in the "world of manifestation" – is their rates of vibration – a different pattern of vibration – producing a different "end-product."[182]

A string so small, it boggles the mind. It is said that the length of a string loop is approximately a hundred billion billion (10^{20}) times smaller than an atomic nucleus. It's hard to conceive of it – even being of this world. Not far different from the finite mind trying to understand the Infinite – the Creator.

Although being such a controversial theory, it shouldn't be long before it's proven absolutely true. For that's the way – it exactly is!

---

182   For a fuller and more enlightening understanding of string theory, have a read of Dr. Brian Greene's books, *The Elegant Universe: Superstrings, Hidden Dimensions, and The Quest for the Ultimate Theory* (New York: Vintage Books, 2000), and *The Fabric of the Cosmos: Space, Time, and the Texture of Reality* (New York: Alfred A. Knopf, 2004).

THE AUM – LIGHT CONNECTION

We have already learned that the Divine and light are synonymous. So if He is present as the omnipresent Christ Consciousness, immanent in the cosmic vibration – Aum; the corollary should logically be that every particle of creation should be composed of light. And this has already been scientifically proven. That is, all manifestations in the physical world have been found to be made up of electromagnetic waves or frozen light.

Isn't it indubitably wonderful how the pieces of creation fit together when we make a super-determined effort to unravel this greatest of mysteries?

THE DIVINE SOUND

Restless breath abating,
Revealed in the stillest mind;
The most sacred sound from which
All others originate –
The omnipresent, eternal, blissful Aum!
Emanating from every
Speck of creation,
Like illimitable beams of light
Radiating from the august sun.
Bringing forth the ultimate realization:
The Originless, Timeless, Divine Sound
Which reverberates fully within
Our awakened consciousness,
Is one with,
And no different from –
Its ubiquitous presence,
In the body of the Most High –
Prakriti, or Mother Nature!

CHAPTER 15 | God The Father

 Knowing now as we do, how creation came into existence, there should be, unquestionably, a perplexing question still lingering in your minds. And that is – Why did the Creator bring the cosmos into manifestation? (Not that it hasn't baffled many of you before, or lingered in the minds of deep thinkers throughout the ages).

According to the great spiritual traditions of the world, as well as those "God-men" who dedicated their lives to self-realization – reuniting their souls with the Divine, and for whom "all" is known. We learn that before this ever-changing panorama of creation, only transcendental, pure, eternal Spirit existed. But for us to truly envision what it was like, we have to imagine we are fast asleep, in a dream. And in that dream, everywhere we look, there is just illimitable space. And that illimitable space is permeated with a joy indescribable, and at the same time, possessing infinite intelligence and, of course, being omnipotent!

With this picture in mind, it becomes a lot easier then to appreciate why the Divine would one "day" think to Himself, *Ah! Only Infinite Self exists, there is no one to enjoy My infinite bliss or My inconceivable wonders. And if I create a cosmos, I could also delight in my myriad manifestations.*

"O Lord...thou hast created all things, and for thy pleasure they are and were created."[183]

A scenario in our human minds that can be likened to an exceedingly wealthy, single person, running a billion dollar empire, having a large number of fantastic mansions – located in the most exotic locales in the world with a vast collection of fast and super expensive cars and a fleet of luxury jets to boot, yet not having a "special one" to share in his incredible good fortune, or indulge in his "excesses." And if he did, at the same time, he would also have the immense pleasure, of seeing the apple of his eye, reveling, in his "fairy-tale" lifestyle. (Which certainly reminds one of the old saying – we live on through our children.) Isn't this also one of the most important reasons why royalty seek so desperately to produce an heir to the throne?

WHO MADE GOD?

A natural "offshoot" of the above-mentioned question, is obviously, who made God? In human terms, we use our mental capacity as the yard-stick to evaluate situations and form opinions. So everything is merely a matter of our own perspective. The man with an inadequate memory believes everyone is in the same boat as he is. But this is not reality at all, as there are numerous people with photographic memories, who can memorize the entire contents of a book; for example, children in Arabic nations are trained to memorize the entire contents of the holy Koran. Or to cite a more common example, imagine a Bedouin who makes his home next to an oasis, whose diet (as you may have guessed) consists mainly of dates. Running into a Hindu, and very curiously inquiring whether dates grow in India. On getting a negative response, he is totally confounded, as he can't come to terms on how, then, does his acquaintance survive.

So to think, then, (using our mortal consciousness) that because we were created, in like manner someone created God, is quite erroneous.

---

183   Rev. 4:11.

"For My thoughts are not your thoughts … so are My ways higher than your ways, and My thoughts than your thoughts."[184]

Or, to view things from a much deeper level – reflect on also your true self (the divine soul cloaked in the transitory body), which is itself uncreated. So if the wave (the soul) was not created,[185] and the pure soul is part and parcel of the ocean (the Divine), then quite obviously Eternal Spirit is uncreated too!

HOW WAS CREATION MANIFESTED?

The ingenious means employed by the Divine in creating the cosmos is exceedingly and unbelievably fascinating. But what makes it more incredible is that we can actually identify with the way it was all done.

After arranging His creative ideas into an utterly structured and logical framework, He then used that Divine blueprint, to dream up a cosmos. As we all know, if we have a thought about that "special one," we cannot see them or have any emotional connection with them, for they are just a mental concept. But on the other hand, if we were to dream about them – a whole new dimension opens; there is now an emotional reality to the experience or a far greater tangible expression of our consciousness. So similarly, to make His thoughts more concrete or real, He "condensed" them into a dream. This is called His lila or cosmic play.

In the same way then, we beings made in His image can do the same in the magical world of dreams. In dreams, we objectify our all-entertaining thoughts, through the power of our imaginations, and so can duplicate any experience of this mundane world. Our senses gain a reality, (missing when we are just lost in thought), our minds, (like when we are awake) have the full capacity to reason; and as strange as it may sound, our souls can actually have experiences through another body. As a matter of fact, if we could only make our dream experiences real to our physi-

---

184   Isaiah 55:8,9.

185   "For the soul there is neither birth nor death at any time. He has not come into being, does not come into being, and will not come into being" (Bhagavad Gita II:20).

cal senses, then we would have done the exact same thing and "created" like the Creator.

But when we are awake, the dreams and their depictions lose their reality, because the subconscious mind, which holds together the fabric of the subconscious thoughts, releases its cohesive bond, withdrawing its life energy, only to be utilized in experiences of our waking consciousness, or in other words, we escape from this state, and realize that we were only dreaming.

Similarly, when we fully awake in Spirit – becoming one with God, and the veils of maya are parted, we'll see all creation as only a cosmic dream or the frozen imaginings of God.

THE COSMIC MOTION PICTURE

Why is the divine lila referred to as the cosmic play? Because, like the showing of a motion picture, in which the continuous beam of light (electricity) from the projector booth creates all the absorbing scenes of tragedy, drama, and comedy on the imageless white screen,[186] in which there is no life and death – just electrical images darting "back and forth." And where the operator does not get emotionally involved in the show taking place before him, having seen it over and over; unlike the enrapt audience fully identifying with the vastly entertaining scenes. Momentarily forgetting they are just images of light.

In the same way creation is a motion picture in which the Divine Light (Cosmic Electricity) projects from the projection booth of God's mind onto the screen of this earth, transforming into the delusive cosmic scenes of endless trials, old age, life, and death that go with birth in the material world. But ultimately, when we "free" ourselves from this cosmic picture show, we will know unequivocally that at the core of our nature we are the rays of that Immortal Light. And that the phenomenal world is nothing more than this divine current, passing through the film of maya.

---

186   Images on a screen (as we all know), are the result of passing a beam of light through a film.

It is extremely worthwhile to remember that we, as both actors and audience, should not become too entangled in the goings-on of this cosmic picture show. But at the same time, to pay heed to the fact that each one's role is as vital to the cosmic play as any other!

HEAVEN ON EARTH

Being made in the image of God; in the "beginning," we were "pure" beings – devoid of sin – vibrating at an extremely high level of consciousness. We were originally to inherit the pristine earth – the perfect paradise – Eden, or heaven on earth. And it was the Divine's plan that we would live in peace and harmony and love (loving each other as brothers, as we are supposed to), enjoying the incredible wonders of creation that were ours to truly enjoy. And eventually, after a period of time, free from evil and sin, we would effortlessly and naturally, like the proverbial prodigal son, return to our true home in Him.

Being omniscient, the Divine was fully aware of our fall from grace, and that His children, cannot be really happy, until they are one with Him again. It takes a severe case of "trials and tribulation" before man awakens. But knowing man; his erring ego, always makes him take the really long way out!

Knowing this perpetual dilemma that would face us in the future, the God-realized yogis of ancient times left us priceless treasures of scientific spiritual techniques, which when practiced wholeheartedly and regularly, decrease the mileage in our journey back to Godhead!

"WOW" FACTORS IN CREATION

There are many who cling inexorably to the belief that the creation of the cosmos is no more than a mere accident, devoid of any participation by a "Higher Force." And that it is due to the most extreme and bizarre atmospheric conditions, billions of years ago, that the first particle of creation originated (the Big Bang theory). Which then gradually evolved into myriad life forms – culminating in the end result – man! What is most extraordinary, though, is that most adherents to this school of thought formed their opinions without really paying attention to, or taking the time to fully investigate, what is actually taking place "behind the scenes," and then seeing whether it's really logical to take such a stance, or not.

In any event, out of literally countless operations simultaneously working harmoniously in nature to keep creation running indefinitely, here are a few select examples, to demonstrate the extraordinary wonders of creation. (1) Although there is an astronomical number of unstationary celestial bodies, yet apart from a few relatively minor collisions (which is utterly natural), there seems to be a definite pattern of order, as there is no evidence of mass collisions taking place. (2) The atomic particles, electrons and protons, have precisely equal and opposite electrical charges, that ensure the stability of all matter. (3) In the process of photosynthesis, plants give off oxygen as a by-product, which we are so desperately in need of to survive. And we in turn, provide carbon dioxide through exhalation; utilized as an essential "raw material" in photosynthesis. (4) Our amazing "army" – the immune system, provides us the vital protection we need when healthy against "invaders." (5) Our fascinating sensory "circuit" continually sends impulses to be analyzed via the sensory nerves to the brain, which then relays responses via the motor nerves, as reactions to its analysis. (6) One of the most efficient pumps in existence, the heart, pumps approximately eighteen tons of blood per day. (7) The human brain is the most sophisticated computer there is, when it is working at full capacity.

Now, try to conceive of an exceptionally large corporation, like let's say, Microsoft, successfully operating for a very, very long period of time without someone at the "helm." Wouldn't that seem really unrealistic though? Surely seems so, doesn't it? Then isn't it even more unrealistic that the smooth running of the universe, which requires an absolutely greater number of complex operations (including those just mentioned), could continue indefinitely with no one overseeing it?

Or, looked at from another angle, even the greatest empires that dominated the planet, such as the Roman, Greek, Babylonian and Egyptian, although having a "guiding intelligence," after a while, lost their supremacy and faded into the background.

There undoubtedly is scientific evidence that points to evolution. But isn't there the possibility too, that it could have been guided by a "Hidden Hand!" Maybe the eye-opening realization that billions of years on earth are just a blink of an eye in the realm of Spirit, or that it is impossible for "unguided" evolution, to bring about the perfect state of duality that exists in creation, may eventually bring about a change of heart!

GOD THE FATHER

I've lived, I've lived, I've lived.
I've died, I've died, I've died.
How many times I've cried.
My fragile heart,
Immersed in delusion
Has splintered into countless pieces,
At losing so many fathers,
O'er the eons of time!

But if my spiritual quest,
Leads to self-realization
The empty spaces in my soul,
Automatically fill up,
I am devoid of no more sorrow!

For I am enchanted to realize,
It was God, the Father,
Who masqueraded in so many forms
To keep me entertained.
Or that in reality
There was never
Really no other, but only
He Himself, all along!

CHAPTER 16

The Astral Planes

 In the luminous astral body, comprising the aforementioned nineteen elements, the indwelling "inhabitant – the soul, heads through the third eye into a tunnel of bright light, to enter the heavenly dimensions.

Irrespective of what may have caused the "casting off" of the mortal shell, whether it be a tragic accident, at the "hands of another," or through a terrible illness. On leaving the body, there is no more pain.

It is enormously helpful that we have a mind-set that we're going home (it's literally so), for those who don't believe in a hereafter,[187] or who become too entangled in the mesh of the material world and do not want to part with their earthly "accumulations," become trapped as strangers (ghosts), in a realm that is no longer their home.

Apart from losing our bodily over-coats, we are essentially the same, with one major difference. Our thoughts are identical, our desires are no different from before, and our habits and character remain unchanged. And we are still wholly conscious of our actions. And that one major difference, is that the elderly no longer have a "worn out" and decrepit appearance, but they look like when they were in the prime of life. (Haven't

---

187   All the great religious traditions of the world instruct us that death is not the be-all and end-all of existence. Evidently then, there must be a place for us to go!

you ever dreamt of an aged parent that "passed away," and they appeared the same?)

Unfortunately then, we don't just become angels by casting off the body. If it were that easy, why don't we all just jump into the ocean, free ourselves from our "burdens," and sit on the "right hand," of our "Maker." Only on earth, are wrinkles of imperfections, ironed out!

MODE OF CONVEYANCE

Now that it is obvious we still have an "existence," after discarding the physical body, and we have a destination, the lingering question becomes: "What might the conveyance be?" In this vastly mystical journey, with no known physical means to give us an inkling. The answer is; our will! We move as fast as light. After all, the astral body is virtually weightless. (Same as in astral projection, the mere thought of being at a location – takes you there, excepting that in this case, you're returning to the same body.) And as already mentioned, if we don't believe in a "destination," then we are "stuck here."

A SEAMLESS TRANSITION

It should be extremely comforting to know our arrival on the "other side" does not involve the customary problems, entailed on our journey to a foreign land on the earthly plane. There is no requirement for identification, we are not faced with the troubling scenario of having to know a foreign language, and our means to obtain things does not depend on having an "item," to exchange to acquire them. (Although in this realm, our actions on earth do play a vital part.)

And for those who have a God-realized guru, their arrival is even more of a cinch. As they will be ushered in by him. For there is a pact in this relationship, where the guru has made a pledge to look over their disciples, life after life, until they reach perfection. (Not unlike cases of near-death experiences, where those whose time did not come reported encountering the form of the deity, they worship, or a close friend, a relative, or a spouse, while out of the body). Isn't it really amazing that in space exploration, astronauts have to be properly equipped to survive in the extremely harsh conditions they must face, yet we in the astral body can travel to another dimension with no requirements for such accoutrements?

MANY MANSIONS

Lord Jesus makes it very clear, heaven is not just one realm, but is actually comprised of many spheres: "In my Father's house are many mansions."[188] It is self-evident that if there were only one plane there would be many mansions to accommodate us all. Hence, a reference to "many mansions," can only mean there are many planes.

Despite the almost seamless transition to our new home, it nevertheless would be very disconcerting and rather confusing, if on arrival we didn't know where to go.

To prevent such a dilemma, we arrive at a central point. From where we are carted off to the Hall of Memories. Where we see a complete replay of our earthly existence, where every secret is told and every experience revealed. We being our sternest judges. We then understandingly select which spiritual lesson we would like to learn when we are born again. Whether it be compassion, forbearance, forgiveness, unconditional love, or wisdom, to name a few. Then, according to our unique ticket, our level of "perfection," or the amount of karma to be worked out, we are sent off to the appropriate plane.

WHAT IS THE NEW HOME LIKE?

Imagine a "land" of exquisite and unimaginable beauty, (which is easily visualized, as we have visited these planes in sleep), not having a care in the world, and having the clear realization of having no fear, that you'll cease to exist. Well, incredibly, this is what it is like for us in our new home.

---

188   John 14:2.

In this realm – there is no existence of contrast or the delusional element of duality. Everything appears in its unalloyed, primordial state.

Here in this finite world there is length, breath, and depth. These limiting measurements, are, however, non-existent in the astral world. In this spiritual dimension, everything is transparent, (just pure consciousness) – a realm of multihued, living light.

Evidently then, being in a realm of light, in a body of light, the way we experience and interact with things is entirely different from the way we do on earth.

There are no bones to be broken, no disease to "strike us down," no sorrow, heartaches, or hardships of any kind. (In fact we are indestructible). Which is more or less part of the "earth experience." Lessons to be learned, to help us become more evolved beings, moving closer towards the "Light."

Since we are now vibrating at an exceedingly higher level (closer to Spirit), all manifestations in this realm are more in harmony with our divine souls, than the cruder vibrations of earthly manifestations. All things exist in mutual helpfulness. So don't expect at any time to run into someone you completely despise or who caused you great distress, or vice-versa. (One of the major reasons we are necessitated to take birth again is to work out issues like these – "human differences" – to learn: all are one). There are no surprises to disrupt the perennial peace and harmony that are inherent to this realm.

Base desires such as lust and wanting to lord it over others don't matter anymore, (they drop into the background of consciousness); only higher values become of relevance.

THE USE OF WILL

The constant harmony is maintained by the fact that we can will into existence any item or condition to replace those that don't suit our fancy. (As a matter of fact) even if you are not pleased with your current appearance (which is the exact replica of your earthly body), you can also will to look like any person, you desire (no plastic surgery).

In this context, if you lived on the edge and like fast cars, you can "dream up" your own model, will it into manifestation, and then travel any distance instantaneously.

If you enjoyed playing sports, you can will into being the "setting" for whatever game you like to play. Everything you need is literally at your fingertips.

And if you simply like the quieter "life," you can create your own special garden, with all the types of flowers that suit your fancy. You can even add a nice quiet brook. And to set the scene just right, add a few oak trees. When we've had enough, we do the opposite and simply dematerialize them. Nothing to be in awe of, though. As we all do this subconsciously in dreams. And when we've realized our true identity, it is easily done at the physical level too.

Incredibly, the extraordinary use of our will is not the only paranormal ability we have at our disposal. Although we can experience sensations through the five astral senses (the counterparts of the physical senses). Because all things are now a pure expression of consciousness, we can actually employ the sixth sense – intuition, to perceive outward stimuli. Or put another way, by sheer intuitional feeling alone – one fulfills the functions of all the five senses. What is really amazing, though, is that any sensation can be experienced through any one of the five senses. That is, we can see through the ear or nose or skin. Or hear through the eyes or nose or tongue etc.

Concomitantly too, we no longer need the spoken word for communication. All "conversing" is done telepathically. One common "language" – the language of Spirit. Communication is now an intimate or sublime exchange of thoughts and feelings. For that matter, everything there talks silently!

As might be expected, those who are more spiritually advanced and residing in the higher vibratory regions, will be blessed with more freedom and a wider range of the use of their will, plus a greater level of appreciation, for their supernal surroundings.

SOME OBJECTIVE DEPICTIONS

To get a better understanding of the unparalleled beauty of this heavenly paradise, picture that everything we stand in awe of on the earthly plane is just an inferior copy of what exists in the heavenly realm. And also, being in the astral body, the range of vibrations we can now perceive with our astral vision (the third eye is now opened), encompasses an enormously vaster range.

There are majestic, iridescent mountains with swirling mists of multi-hued, radiant light; amazing unpolluted lakes, rivers, and oceans of soul-harmonic tranquility, which give reflections of a variety of scintillating, dazzling, enchanting colours and are teeming with fishes of indescribable beauty, plus other life forms (counterparts of those found on the material plane, including, what many believe to be mythical – the mermaid).[189] It is utterly fascinating that with all these forms, that mermaids are included. Because growing up, no one believed the remarkable tale my aunt swore by, of seeing a mermaid basking in the sun, combing her long, beautiful, blond hair, lying on a rock at the water's edge. (And they still don't). There are also lush, green forests, where the flora exist in a mutually beneficial relationship. And to go with all that, instead of the continually changing seasons and weather conditions that we have on the earth plane, there is an idyllic weather system, with springlike conditions – "all year round."

Obviously too, everyone will have their dream dwelling, garnished with their dream furniture, brought into manifestation by the power of their imaginative will.

---

189   See *Autobiography of a Yogi*: chapter 43, page 459; where Yogananda's resurrected guru, Sri Yukteswar, describes the astral planes.

DIETARY REQUIREMENTS

Because we now have different bodies, our dietary requirements, as one surely might expect, will be entirely different.

Instead of gross foods and liquid "quenchers," our diet will now solely consist of multihued rays of light (no digestive problems), which we can will to duplicate the taste of any earthly flavor. (Although there are fountains, giving a "heavenly" nectar we can imbibe, or vegetables of light that can be procured from below the ground, if we need extra variety.)

It is not a mere metaphoric reference then, in the great scriptures of the world, that we partake of ambrosia or food of the Gods, in the afterlife – it is actually so. For having the ability to create by will, many do create tastes that are "not of this world," or they can simply get a different tasting one, from the magical fountains.

WILL WE MEET OUR LOVED ONES?

In reality, there is a strong possibility that we will see our loved ones when we leave this world. But there is no guarantee. Because that all depends on whether they have reincarnated again, or whether they will be on the same plane we'll be delegated to in "passing on."

In any event, although we continuously think of our departed ones and look forward ever-so-longingly to reunite with them, when we ourselves "depart," it's not as perturbing as you might think, if we don't.

Because, while in the astral planes, we have the clear realization of the delusional nature of the physical world, and that in reality – all souls are one. So there is hardly, really anything to miss. Is it not?

To crown it all off, we are welcomed with wide open arms into families that vibrate on the same level as us, where we experience great love, genuine joy, and continuous harmony. (There are none of those ups and downs we generally encounter with an earthly family).

Only because of the cosmic play where we see ourselves playing different roles, does it seem that we are connected to a limited family.

THE HIGHEST REALM

There is even still a higher dimension than the astral planes, where almost-perfect souls (having only the "thinly" created causal overcoat, embodying the soul), reside. That is the causal planes. But "residences" become superfluous when we rid ourselves of our three overcoats (the physical, astral, and causal bodies), and merge with Transcendent Spirit. In which case, we can remain as such, or join the divine hierarchical team in running the universe. We can be assigned to any plane, like Sri Yukteswar, who was directed by the Divine to serve on the high astral plane of Hiranyaloka,[190] where only those who have "conquered death" (leaving the body consciously, owing to having attained an exceedingly high state of spiritual development), can go. Where he assists those who have redeemed their earthly karma and do not return to the earth plane, work out traces of astral karma, so that they can elevate to the higher causal realm (then having just a little causal karma to work out, subsequently becoming one with Spirit).[191] Or assist beings leaving earth, arriving on the ordinary astral spheres, with their life reviews and preparation for their next earthly incarnation.

Or if he is delegated for a real "special job," the God-realized being puts on the physical overcoat and returns to "teach" – which we refer to as an avatar.

LENGTH OF STAY IN THE ASTRAL WORLD

There should be no fear of death, then, if you can see you are going to a much higher dimension, much closer to your true nature than it is while on the earthly plane. It's natural to miss our loved ones and possessions we struggled so hard to obtain. But for what it's worth, being free from all physical discomfort, in a youthful, highly energized body, and looking forward to meeting beings who will be "vibrating at the same level" as

---

190 This information is revealed in chapter 43 (page 457) of *Autobiography of a Yogi*.
191 This takes some doing, though–this already being a very high heaven, the residents see no real necessity to make a strenuous effort in trying to move up to an even higher realm.

you (including a familiar face or two), should surely make it a case where the pros heavily outweigh the cons.

In any event, the length of stay is not the same for everyone. It is karmically determined. So long as we have unfulfilled material desires or earthly karma to be redeemed (effects of actions not worked out), we must reincarnate on earth to continue our evolution back to Godhead.

However, the ideal conditions are not always present immediately, for us to enact our role in the next life. It takes a while for every detail to be matched, so that the inexorable law of karma is satisfied (as already discussed in chapter four).

It is indeed rather amazing, that although we have been to a "land," where there is no unwilling death, disease, or old age and there are continuous peace and harmony and far superior pleasures to be experienced, yet somehow we are repeatedly drawn back to the earthly plane, which can be considered to be nothing but the opposite, and is in fact – the only true hell!

THE ASTRAL PLANES

The astral planes are truly my home,
Worldly temptations and attachments
Have given me the uncontrollable desire,
To return to the world of matter,
For yet another round.

Irrespective of being there,
Numerous times, too many to count.
And subconsciously know,
That it is there,
Where I do belong.

Yet the tremendous force of my senses
Sways the power of will,
Whichever so subtly,
Is always striving
To make me, eternally free.

But at last, one day
When delusion's head,
Becomes too unbearable to face,
My inner divine strength,
Will work "over-time,"
To make sure
I will not return to earth,
No! not evermore!

CHAPTER 17 | The Science of Chanting

 The science of chanting is one that is as old as the first efforts made by man to seek favours from the Divine, or at a much deeper level – to try to unite with Him.

But more importantly, the singular reason for the inclusion of a chapter on the subject, is to point out that it is a very simple, convenient, yet powerful technique a person can use to make significant progress on his spiritual journey. And when he has reached a certain stage, he will meet his guru, who will take him the rest of the way.

In fact, several religious traditions incorporate chanting as part of their spiritual practice. For example, we are all familiar with the chanting of the Hail Mary prayer on a rosary, in Catholicism; in Tibetan Buddhism they also use a rosary to intone the very profound words Aum mani padme Hum;[192] in Islam, Allaho Akbar, Alhamdulillah, and Subhanallah[193] are regularly repeated a specific number of times. But it is in Hinduism that

---

192 A literal translation being: Hail to the Jewel in the Lotus, (which at a much deeper level means, Hail to the divine spark within).

193 Which mean respectively; God is the greatest, all praise is due to God, and Glory be to God.

chanting plays a much more prominent role. With the Gayatri mantra[194] being one of the most common chants.

THE POWER OF SOUND VIBRATION

The efficacy and consciousness-expanding ability of chanting are the result of the latent power inherent within sound vibration. But this is nothing new, as most of us are familiar with the fact that the pitch of certain sounds can cause a glass to shatter into innumerable pieces. As when a certain note is played on a violin, it results in a wine glass being completely disintegrated.

Also, (although sounding incredible), it is a known fact that a large group of soldiers marching in unison will almost invariably break forma-tion when crossing a bridge. For the single reason that although a bridge is built sturdy enough to withstand the force of a convoy of army trucks, or a fleet of tanks, yet when it comes to soldiers marching in time its stability becomes compromised. And that's because the vibration set up by this movement creates such an explosive force that it causes bridges to come crashing down.

And lastly, we find an even more fascinating example in the holy Bible.

In ancient times, a few thousand years ago, when the Israelites entered the Promised Land (after being freed from Egypt), Jerico[195] was the first town they laid eyes on. But to their utter dismay, the entire perimeter was surrounded by massive walls.

Their fears were soon put to rest, however, when Joshua (their leader), was instructed by the Divine how to solve the dilemma. And what an ingenious and spectacular means it was. He was told to have the people circumambulate the structure once every day, for six days, (while carrying the ark), with the priests blowing their trumpets. But to be increased to seven times, on the seventh day. Followed by loud shouting. And when

---

194   One of the most sacred verses in the Vedas (Rg III, 62:10), used for invoking wisdom in daily living.

195   An ancient town in Jordan.

this was accomplished, without the least resistance the wall came crumbling down. The result of a mighty vibration, that emulated a modern day explosive.[196]

THE MANTRA

As most are well aware, the "tool" one utilizes in chanting is called – a mantra. A word originating from the ancient Sanskrit language meaning: instrument of thought. (The focusing of thought being the key to bringing into being one's conscious intent. It should be no wonder then that psychologists believe a man becomes what he thinks.) It can be a syllable, a word, a sentence, and sometimes even a verse. And represents some particular aspect of the Divine, or a direct plea for "spiritual awakening." But should not be confused with worldly sounds, for they are transcendental sound vibrations. This uncomplicated branch of metaphysics is often referred to as mantra yoga or meditation, or japa yoga.

One of the more common mantras used to attain self-realization is the divine sound, you've come to be so familiar with – Aum or Om. Other, just as potent, mantras include; Aum Nama[197] Shivaya, Aum Sai Ram, Ram or Rama,[198] and probably one of the most recognizable – the maha[199] or Hare[200] Krishna mantra.

Chanting is simple, because there really is no specific way it should be done. It can be done loudly, quietly, mentally, and even within a group (kirtan) – where a leader utters the mantra first, followed by other members of the group.

---

196 Joshua 6:1-16, 20.

197 Nama means name. Used in the mantra to differentiate between the personal and impersonal God. Seeing chanting involves the Divine with form, "Nama" is included as part of the chant.

198 An avatar who lived thousands of years ago. And whose life is recorded in the Hindu epic – the Ramayana. (Mentioned in chapter four).

199 A word meaning great, in Sanskrit.

200 Which means: Oh energy of the Lord.

It is convenient because it can be done privately at home, while walking outdoors, while waiting for the bus, or when just casually relaxing by the beach or in the park.

Although ideally it is best if it can be done at home. Using a set of beads, doing one or two rounds at a specific time in the morning and afternoon. And then gradually working up to a higher level you are comfortable with. (It is said doing your spiritual practice in the same place, permeates the spot with holy vibrations, and makes it easier every time to get into a God-attuned frame of mind).

One can also find it very beneficial to do some soulful chanting when the mind is restless, or you need to get some relief from worry or negative thoughts.

PROOF OF EFFICACY

The potency of chanting is evidenced by the fact that in the world of God-realized men, there are many who have attained enlightenment, solely by the practice of japa meditation.

And for some, their rich legacies still live on in the ashrams they established, which are run by their devout devotees, who have been initiated[201] on the spiritual path by the passing on of the exact same mantra used by their gurus, to attain self-realization. With many achieving the goal, for which this sacred tool, was transmitted.

(However, the spiritual environment of the ashram, accompanied by the disciplined life the devotees live, and the ever-watchful eye of their deathless gurus, nevertheless do make their journey to self-realization a lot easier than for those attempting this inevitable journey on their own).

The master (Yogi Ramsuratkumar 1918-2001), mentioned in chapter eleven, merged with the Heavenly Father solely by the chanting of Lord Rama's name, as did his great guru – Swami Ramdas 1884-1963, (also known as Papa Das). Their ashrams are still operational today. Both are

---

201 An initiation that usually involves the passing on of the mantra at a special ceremony, in which the master-disciple bond is formed, by the former whispering the mantra into the ear of the latter.

located in the south of India, and they are known as Yogi Ramsuratkumar Ashram, and Anandashram respectively.

And because his name is world renowned, recognized by millions to have attained self-realization, it should be pointed out that the Mahatma (Ghandi) built almost his entire spiritual foundation on the divine name – Rama (his mantra since youth). Hence, it is no mere coincidence that it was the last word[202] uttered from his dying lips, after being shot five times. (Unfortunately, his ashram is no longer a spiritual center, but a tourist attraction, instead).

A TALE FOR ALL TIMES

But this section of the chapter would not be complete if the utterly re-markable story of A. C. Bhaktivedanta Swami Prabhupada were not told.

Entrusted with a sacred mission by his spiritual master[203] in 1922, in Calcutta, India. He crossed the Atlantic at the ripe old age of almost seventy, (suffering two heart attacks on the way), arriving in America in the late summer of 1965, with nothing but a few dollars, an umbrella, a single suitcase, and a few copies of the translation and purports of the early chapters of Shrimad-Bhagavatam.[204]

He began a worldwide spiritual movement – ISKCON[205] (still going strong today) in virtually every corner of the world. With many of their temples being so magnificent that they're fit for royalty. And he did it all by introducing to his congregations, the already mentioned, well known Hare Krishna mantra.[206] (Getting started in a very small storefront, pro-

---

202   "And whoever, at the end of life, quits his body remembering Me alone, at once attains My nature. Of this there is no doubt" (Bhagavad Gita VIII:5). This is not as simple as it might seem. Only one accustomed to having the Divine Name on his lips throughout life can effortlessly recall It at the extremely traumatic time of passing.

203   Bhaktisiddhanta Sarasvati Thakura.

204   The Hindu epic of which the Bhagavad Gita, is but a part.

205   International Society for Krishna Consciousness.

206   Hare Krishna, Hare Krishna, Krishna Krishna, Hare Hare, Hare Rama, Hare Rama, Rama Rama, Hare Hare.

cured for him by some very generous, new acquaintances. Some of whom, later became his disciples.)

Was it the hand of destiny or coincidence, though, that brought him to the Lower East side of New York City, where the counter-culture revolution was taking place. Where the disgruntled middle-class youth (the "peace and love" crowd) of the nation were rebelling against society, looking for the ultimate truth and expanding their consciousness with mind-altering "substances." And willing to experiment with any new method to do so. With the chanting of the Hare Krishna mantra, they were wildly surprised to find there was no coming down from this high. And in fact, with each successive "high," the effects were only cumulative. Ultimately opening the mystical door to self-realization.

It is no surprise then, that many of the swami's early disciples came from the counter-culture movement. Although this could have been no easy commitment, as it entailed being a vegetarian; no imbibing of alcoholic beverages; no gambling; and no sex outside of marriage (even that being regulated). And which naturally involved the chanting of the mantra a specified number of times daily.

Incidentally, it should be mentioned that two members of a British super group (no longer with us), who experienced the ecstatic effects of chanting the maha mantra, once chanted it quite regularly for a few days as they sailed through the Greek Islands, with one session being as long as six hours.

ENLIGHTENMENT NOT LIMITED TO A FEW DISCIPLINES

In no way should one get the impression that self-realization is limited to just a few disciplines. In fact, there are numerous paths. Even in yoga, there are several different branches such as; karma, jnana, raja, laya, and bhakti yoga.[207]

---

207 Karma yoga involves doing good works and participation in right activity; jnana yoga is the attainment of enlightenment through knowledge; raja yoga is a system of body discipline, combined

NOT SECRET MANTRAS

It's rather comical indeed, when some of us may have heard about mystics or ascetics secludedly chanting in some cave or dense forest, attaining all types of supernormal powers (although they seldomly use them for selfish purposes), and quizzically wonder what kind of highly secretive or extremely magical mantra they might be using. When in fact, it's just the Divine name, or some aspect of His nature, they are constantly repeating.

WE'RE ALWAYS CHANTING

In reality, life itself is one continuous chant, for with each inhalation and exhalation of the breath, we make the almost inaudible, characteristic sounds of So and Ham respectively. Which when combined, comprise the Sanskrit word, Soham, which when translated into English literally means, "I am He." And it would be of invaluable benefit to remember, because of the subtle, mysterious power of sound, everything we say affects the chakras. Hence eliminating negativity and unpleasantness in our speech can only mean we are reducing steps we have to make on our journey to God-realization!

---

with an extremely potent meditative technique; laya yoga is the total focusing of the mind on any mental aspect of the Divine, or inner astral sound; and bhakti yoga is total devotion to a self-realized guru, truth, or the Divine.

THE SCIENCE OF CHANTING

The science of chanting
Is a potent spiritual practice,
One of many, available to us,
To travel the seemingly endless:
Highway of mortality—
Destination – ultimately: Divinity!

With the simplest of tools—
A word or two—
Called a mantra,
To make the goal, a reality!

But make no mistake,
Like any great undertaking,
This, the "mother of undertakings"
Requires a super strong,
And indomitable will!
To cover the gargantuan mileage,
On this spiritual journey!

CHAPTER 18 | Questions and Answers

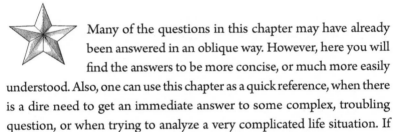 Many of the questions in this chapter may have already been answered in an oblique way. However, here you will find the answers to be more concise, or much more easily understood. Also, one can use this chapter as a quick reference, when there is a dire need to get an immediate answer to some complex, troubling question, or when trying to analyze a very complicated life situation. If pondered over for a few minutes, with unclouded judgement, one most undoubtedly will get assurance from that part within us – that is truth itself.

So, here goes!

Question: Why don't I just stick to my traditional religious beliefs?

Answer: This is as good a question, as it gets. As the majority of religionists fall into this category. However, in this case, the emphasis is almost entirely placed on the "outside" world where everything appears separate and distinct, with no direction to our divine connection within. Where we can have a practical and concrete experience of the Divine (seeing One in all, and all in One), instead of following a path, totally based on theological dogma. Doesn't one wonder how many in this group are unbiased to other religious traditions? When all lead to the same goal, but in a different way. Or how many treat their fellow human beings as they would like to be treated? These things are supposed to be realities when we follow our traditional teachings, but somehow, they're not. Hence, there seems to be a very strong discrepancy here!

However, if one were to follow the commandments of their scriptures, and pursue their spiritual practices, as outlined in their holy texts, surely they would make great strides on their spiritual journey. Just think how many of us are really one-pointed in prayer (being able to control the numberless thoughts bombarding our minds) – the way it should be, when we offer our devotions.

Simply put, it's just that in the journey to Godhead, saints, and sages have found quicker ways to attain the same goal. (But in no way, should one think that they cannot continue with their spiritual tradition if they practice a scientific method of meditation. In fact, it will only greatly enhance our devotion, in our act of worship).

Question: Why is God indifferent to human suffering?

Answer: In His mind, there is no suffering – it is all His lila – His cosmic play: like waking up from a dream that seems so real, and realizing it was illusional. Or if viewed from another angle, if He were to intercede, we might be prone to making the same mistake again that caused our suffering, in the first place. As we might have not thoroughly learned the lesson we were supposed to, from that painful experience. (In effect, impeding our progress on the spiritual path. Meaning that the experience will have to be repeated again.) After all, it is all karmically fated, not divinely willed.

Question: Should I fear death?

Answer: Why fear death? It is just fear of the unknown that causes us great dread. On exiting the body, we're "exactly" the same—unhurtable and disassociated from it – vibrating at a much faster level. (Let's just say it's like waking up from a normal, deep sleep, but when you realize it – there is no body!) It would help tremendously if we knew where we are headed to, though!

Question: Will the world be coming to an end anytime soon?

Answer: Well! First of all, an end is inevitable. As everything in the physical world has its opposite. That is, what has a beginning, ultimately has an end – the inexorable law of duality or polarity. But it shouldn't even be something that crosses our minds. As according to the great masters (also corroborated by the ancient Vedic texts), it is so infinitely far into the future, the astronomical figure would actually boggle the mind. (However, there cannot be peace without war, or harmony without disharmony). So naturally, there will always be periods of great disaster as long as the world continues to exist. Although, in the time span of the Satya Yuga, this will be reduced to the barest minimum.

Also, we need this earth-stage to continually play our parts in our journey to mergence with the Divine. Further substantiating the continued existence of the world.

Question: Can a man be reborn as a woman?

Answer: The temporary overcoat we wear identifies us with gender. However, the immortal spark of divinity within, is genderless. Sometimes to learn a special lesson in our incarnations, it is not uncommon to switch genders. Hence in life, we may encounter instances of one gender, having strong tendencies of the other.

Question: Why don't we remember past lives?

Answer: For those buying into the doctrine of reincarnation, no doubt this is probably a burning question that invariably passes through one's mind. Beginning, let's say if we can't remember what we had for dinner on a specific day several months ago. Or, the "important" events that took place on a specific day six months ago. Wouldn't it be logical to conclude that to recall living a past life would be almost an impossibility? Although there are lightning-flash instances when we sometimes make a connection of a present-life moment with one from the "past." Which in most cases, is what déjà vu is.

That being said, even more importantly, this is an utterly ingenious ploy employed by the Divine Hand, Itself, to save us from untold heartache.

Can you imagine what it would be like if we could recall all our countless spouses, siblings, parents, offspring, and tons of other relatives? It would be an absolute test of will just trying to figure out who we should really love when we take into consideration our loved ones in our present incarnation. Or, if we had to remember all our experiences with pain and suffering, complete failures, and other terribly agonizing moments, or traumatic ways we died. It really would put an immense damper on our spirits; enough to cripple our will to go on in our present lives.

Then again, if we remembered all our loved ones from all our past incarnations. It would only become more increasingly difficult to expand our love to include all humanity, realizing that each is an identical spark from the Eternal Flame. Which is something we will eventually have to learn to do. So the Divine, by implementing this screen to our past lives, gives us a new slate, so at least we don't have unnecessary dark clouds hanging over our heads to impede our gradual evolution back to being Divine Spirit!

Question: Why do we have to die?

Answer: Everything that lives dies. All manifestations in the material world have opposites. That's just the phenomenal world, though. The bodily overcoat is discarded at the "time of passing." But our eternal essence – the soul, is absolutely indestructible, and we realize, when we are out of the body – we're actually Spirit!

Question: Will my family incarnate with me when I come again?

Answer: It all depends on the unresolved issues and the karma that have to be worked out between the parties. But it has been found (through past-life regressions and documented cases of reincarnation), that it is not uncommon for family members to incarnate with you, although the relationship is not always the same. For example, an offspring from a previous life could be our parent in the current one, or a parent from a former life could be our offspring in this one.

The other scenario is if while on earth our loved ones who have departed have also returned to the phenomenal world, but not as members of our family. Then if we still have a very strong love for them. They will be instinctively drawn into our realm of existence. And we feel that strong connection, once again.

Question: Who am I?

Answer: We are essentially beings of eternal light, who have forgotten our true nature. By continually inhabiting a physical body, our soul has lost its connection with its Source and fully believes itself, to be of a corporeal nature.

The singular reason for including this question is that men throughout the ages have repeatedly asked the question in an intense process of self-inquiry, which alone, ultimately led them to self-realization. Probably the most well-known master to have done so is Sri Ramana Maharshi[208] (1879-1950), whose ashram (Ramanashram), still exists at the foot of the sacred Arunachala mountain, in the city of Tiruvannamali in southern India.

The point of the whole spiritual exercise is that by continually posing the question, "Who am I?" our identity with the false "I" that identifies with the ego, or mortal body consciousness, gradually dissolves, and the true "I" (I Am That I Am)[209]—our essential, divine nature, is ultimately revealed!

He often times asked those seeking spiritual counsel to try to analyze how come in deep sleep they had no awareness of the body, nor of even having a gender. Yet when awake, who is it that fully recognizes that in the state of deep sleep the mind was completely void of thoughts – super rejuvenated, and almost blissful. It was no other than the ever-alert, ever-conscious, egoless consciousness, or pure consciousness of the soul!

---

208 Maharshi means great sage.
209 Exodus 3:14.

Question: If we were created by a Divine Power. Who created that Power?

Answer: Erroneously because we were created, it is not unnatural to think, *Well then, who created our Creator?* It's a simple misunderstanding of comparing our way of thinking with the latter's. Lower species, such as those in the animal kingdom, don't have the power to reason, so quite obviously they are not even exposed to the process of thinking. Likewise, we should not think what applies to us, applies to the Creator. After all – He is not the same "design" as ourselves. We are finite – and He is Infinite.

It should help to realize too, it is all a cosmic play (lila) – a dream in the mind of the Universal Consciousness. It's just because of the veil of maya that we believe we were created!

From a much more profound standpoint, spirit is self-sustaining – beginningless, endless, causeless. The law of causation is only applicable to what is manifested by the Divine Hand. This divine law does not apply to the One who created it.[210] As outlined previously in the volume, time, space, duality (the world of opposites), come into being because of the law of causation – a reality of our mortal consciousness, they are not inherent to Spirit – Cosmic Consciousness. So how then can we even begin to try to figure out who created God, or to think we are subjected to the same laws, as Eternal Spirit!

Question: What really is meditation?

Answer: The art of meditation is rather a misunderstood subject. In the minds of many, it is a simple practice – a quick fix that produces fantastic wonders to the self, in a short period of time. However, this is quite understandable, for unless one is a disciple or exposed to the soul-awakening teachings of a self-realized guru, it becomes no fault of man when he gets a myriad of very basic definitions and methods of practice from literature authored by men of little spiritual realization.

In any event, the true meaning is: Meditation is the one-pointed focusing of the mind and consciousness, to attain communion and ultimate

---

210 Lord Krishna attests to this in the Gita – IV:6 – "Although I am unborn … transcendental form."

union with the Divine! Or viewed from a more simplistic angle, "real meditation" is an incredibly "speeded-up" process, compared to other spiritual methods, in the progress of the soul towards reunion with the Source! (Man can use his mind to concentrate on any object. But only concentration on God, is called meditation.)

Like every other practice that takes time and discipline to master, this is no different. And when considering what the goal is (expanding our limited mortal consciousness to unlimited Divine Consciousness), it's natural to expect these to be multiplied by a factor of many, many times.

Question: If we develop supernormal powers (siddhis) through spiritual efforts, can we use them for self-interest – like winning the lottery?

Answer: In the general sense, most people who come to possess supernormal powers have utterly no need to use them for their own ends. For to attain them, they would have had to reach a very high level of spiritual development, in which they realize the divine nature of the soul and the delusionary nature of the material world. The result of which – there is no more ego (that creates the need for self-interest), and the putting to rest of virtually all earthly desires. And also, they know they cannot unnecessarily disrupt the harmonious plan put in place by the Divine, by interfering with mass or personal karma.

In fact, eight divine qualities become manifest in the man who becomes self-realized. Without enumerating them all. Here are a few examples; the ability to become as large or small as required, satisfying all desires, bringing anything under control, and to be able to materialize anything, he so desireth.[211]

It is no surprise, then, to find these powers only become available to those who are at all times fully in control of them. Another reason being, if the body and mind are not well prepared to handle the tremendous divine energy being channeled – when we acquire such powers, it would be like sending thousands of watts through a hundred-watt bulb.

---

211   Recorded in *The Holy Science,* pages 94 and 95.

But there have been cases where divine powers have been grossly misused. Unfortunately, those who have done so eventually "fall from grace," plus they suffer very severe penalties for breaking cosmic laws. Not unlike when we break laws in society, we have to pay penalties, some as we know – being very serious!

Question: Are there intelligent life forms other than the human species?

Answer: According to the self-realized masters,[212] and the Hindu Bible – the Bhagavad Gita,[213] we are not the only intelligent life forms in creation. But if we think of it, our limited range of experience is just a very minute part of the incredibly vast cosmos. Isn't it? And the astounding evidence compiled over the years points to the fact – that they might have even more advanced technologies than ours. As evidenced by the amazing crafts they travel in.

But being part of material creation, they are subject to the laws of duality also. And sooner or later, must…give up their bodies too.[214] Interestingly enough, we ourselves may have lived on an extraterrestrial plane, some time or the other. But what is most important here, is that only in a human body can the individualized soul reunite with Godhead. So consider how very fortunate we are!

Finally, one last point on the subject, and that is the existence of extraterrestrials will become common knowledge in a decade, or two!

Question: Is it too late to start the spiritual journey?

Answer: Absolutely not, we have to start it some time. Procrastinating only means we're preventing ourselves from greatly speeding up the process on a journey we were put on this earth, to undertake.

---

212 See *Man's Eternal Quest,* page 287. Also, *Astrology, The Supernatural And The Beyond* by Sri Chinmoy. Jamaica, New York: Agni Press, 1973; page 103.

213 "…the Manus (progenitors of mankind) come from Me, born from My mind, and all the living beings populating the various planets descend from them" (X:6).

214 "From the highest planet in the material world down to the lowest, all are places of misery wherein repeated birth and death take place" (Bhagavad Gita VIII:16).

But more importantly, what may seem like a long, arduous road, may not be so. For more than a few earnest "beginners," have found that progress was not slow in the coming. Because they had travelled many miles on their journey in a previous incarnation, and making the first step was just a continuation of what was started, before.

It is evident that doing what we were born to do can only mean there will be an absolutely great sense – of inner satisfaction!

THE QUESTION

To ask a very profound question,
Is to expand the mind.
If the answer is not satisfactory,
Don't give up—
Simply try another time!
There's no question,
Without a true answer.
Although sometimes, it's hard to find!
Contemplate on this:
In this world of polarity,
In which we exist—
There's nary one single thing,
Without its natural antithesis.
So the same goes, for a question,
A genuine answer, there must be!
And so, should not be left dangling,
In limbo, without reason, or rhyme!

| The Final Spin

 The concept of man's inseparateness from his "Maker" is not the workings of someone with an overactive imagination.

In fact, it only seems fictional because so many are caught up in delusion, fully magnetized to the lures of the material world, it becomes quite difficult to distinguish what is real and what is not. Because wholly identifying with the body ("the egoic principle"), leaves no room to discover – we are a spark of Divinity – the soul. And not entirely our fault also, as we have learned that karma, Yugas, and "birth signs" play a part in some way or the other, with regards to our proclivity for real profound – "spiritual matters."

In a way, the mysteries of creation are somewhat of an esoteric matter, and there is good reason for it being so. It's more or less common knowledge that the incredible stories now being told about "strange flying objects," abductions, and ghosts would have had to be bolted up inside by those who have experienced them, not so long ago. Unless of course, they wanted to be carted off, in a straight jacket, or to be isolated from those close to them because of being categorized, as being nothing short, of "missing a few marbles."

In the same way, when men throughout the ages could not be fully satisfied by mere faith in scriptural texts and set about with absolute resolve to unravel the great mysteries of creation by journeying inwards. (But make no mistake – more than a few got their cues from the scriptural texts.). Upon attaining self-realization, they dared not speak without caution about their revelations, for it would have amounted to nothing less than extreme heresy. And we all know what their fates would have been. And the second, and just as important reason, for making their revelations and experiences available only to their close followers (disciples) is that in this way, their teachings are guaranteed to be preserved in their true form, as otherwise they would be distorted, if they were presented to those not mentally, physically, spiritually, and karmically prepared to receive such absolutely divine knowledge.

Nevertheless, although it's really a very slow process, with each passing day as the sun heads back in the direction towards Vishnunabhi (as discussed in chapter ten), be assured that this can only mean that more "light" is coming into the world, and slowly but surely, more and more of mankind will be waking up to the reality – of their divine status. (And if one looks deeply, it will become apparent, as compared to several decades ago, that there are clear signs to this end.)

FEW AND FAR BETWEEN

In the meantime, we should ponder very deeply. If all men are made equal, and some have attained God-realization (although few and far between), this can only mean we have fallen behind. Is it not? And the more we procrastinate, it's logical that we are just delaying the inevitable – wandering aimlessly, in delusion.

Truth cannot be circumscribed, it will always be out there, and just like how radio and television "waves" are "picked up" when we have sets that can tune in to their frequencies (before making them perceptible to us), similarly when the consciousness frequency of our minds are at the right level, they will "pick up" the truth[215] also. It's a simple matter, really – everything is just a matter of how our individual minds conceive of it.

---

215 "And ye shall know the truth, and the truth shall make you free" (John 8:32).

Think of it. If inquiring minds had not taken the time and effort to prove that the earth was really round and rotating around the sun. We would still be believing that it was flat and maybe some of us might fall off of it. The underlying point, obviously of course, is that to unravel great truths, needs great and continuous investigational efforts!

THE CONTINUOUSLY ROTATING WHEEL OF BIRTH AND DEATH

The doctrine of reincarnation is an absolute reality, to the man of God-realization. And whether it may seem incredible or not. There are numerous such beings present on earth at this time.

Chapter four may have made true believers of some in this not-so-universal doctrine, also.

Now, if there is a just, and unconditionally loving Divine Being, in whose image we are made, and at the same time there is the continuously rotating wheel of birth and death.[216] A scenario that can be considered to be nothing short of being absolutely tortuously repetitive (so much so, that we would not wish this upon the most unrighteous of persons), with its stages of a playful childhood, our educational period, earning a living, raising a family, our golden years, and finally – "dreadful" death.

(Not to mention interspersed with painful episodes of injury, disease, and sorrow.)

It would seem to be the most nonsensical thing that would be done by Him. One possessing absolute Wisdom. (Which for all intents and purposes would be an utter impossibility.) Unless, of course, there has to be an ultimate resolution to this seemingly endless round of death and rebirth. And when will that be? And the only logical answer is – when

---

216   In this context, there is the incredible case of a devotee who was brought back to life by Sai Baba. For the period outside his physical body, the devotee described being in the astral world, in the Hall of Justice or The Hall of Memories, alongside his divine guru. Who asked that all the records of the devotee's lives be brought to him. And in his lives' reviews, the devotee was able to see lives and lives lived in the past, in lands, that haven't existed for thousands of years. Excerpt from: *Sai Baba: The Holy Man And The Psychiatrist* by Samuel H. Sandweiss – pages 101-103.

we return, to being one with God! – the material which constitutes the essence of this volume!

YE ARE GODS!

The Raja of Venkatagiri[217] and his family were some of the earliest and closest disciples of Sai Baba in the late 1940s. And one day, the Raja's younger son asked their divine guru, "What is it that makes you different from other great spiritual masters such as Sri Aurobindo and Sri Ramana Maharshi?"[218]

And Baba said, "Through their intense spiritual practices, they reached Godhead." But that with him, he had come as a perfected being; an avatar, where no spiritual "work" was necessary.[219] And again, in a hand-written message to his close devotees, Baba boldly declared "You are the God of this universe."[220]

This overt attestation to our latent divinity (and whose awakening sure seems the purpose for which we were created) is not as secret as one might think, as we find its corroboration more than a few times, in the great scriptural texts.

In addressing the Jews in the temple in Jerusalem, who were angry at him for declaring He was the son of God, Jesus proclaimed, "Is it not written in your law, I said, Ye are Gods?"[221] This striking Biblical quote can hardly seem to portray any ambiguous meaning. Because this proclamation, "Ye are gods" can only mean we are gods or our very nature is no different from divinity. And if we look at our ordinary selves, nothing seems further from the truth, because man by nature is self-centered, lacks compassion, is possessed of great anger, doesn't "care much" for

---

217 One of the princely states in pre-independent India.

218 The latter already mentioned in chapter eighteen. The former, a world renowned "holy man" (1870-1950), whose legacy lives on in his ashram (Sri Aurobindo ashram), located in southern India.

219 Documented in *Miracles Are My Visiting Cards: An Investigative Report On The Psychic Phenomena Associated With Sathya Sai Baba* by Erlendur Haraldsson. London, England: Century Hutchinson Ltd., 1987. Page 85.

220 See, *Sai Baba: The Holy Man And The Psychiatrist* by Samuel H. Sandweiss, page 104.

221 John 10:34.

his neighbor, and the list goes, on and on! It's absolutely understand-able God is a perfect being. So obviously, we are not currently express-ing this reality. And also, as we all know, this could not be a reference to the body, because it is not eternal, but of a transient nature. Hence it becomes quite evident. It is a state to be won, a state still unreached. No other than the wave becoming the Ocean, or our individual mortal consciousness, becoming Universal or Cosmic Consciousness! We find the Christ proclaiming that the individual spark of divinity within him – had attained that state. "I and my Father are one."[222]

In as much as we know that the divine Christ referred to himself as the son of God. Isn't it utterly amazing that there is also this Biblical quote: "Behold what manner of love the Father hath bestowed upon us that we should be called the sons of God."[223] Again pressing home this most profound point, of our divine nature. Which, of course, is yet, to be awakened. The Christ also proclaimed, "Be ye therefore perfect, even as your Father which is in heaven is perfect.[224]

This next Biblical quote sheds light on our latent divinity from a much different angle: "To him that overcometh will I grant to sit with me in my throne, even as I also overcame and am set down with my Father in His throne."[225]

This indicates the qualification (overcoming delusion of being mortal) for attaining the same status as the Christ – who "overcame" and sits on the throne.

For someone "allowed" to sit on a worldly throne, obviously he has to have the right prerequisite – to be of a royal blood-line. Is it not? The same holds true with the heavenly throne: When we "overcome," by becoming God-realized. The only difference here is that we become of a blood-line, of a divine kingdom!

---

222 John 10:30.
223 1 John 3:1.
224 Matt. 5:48.
225 Rev. 3:21.

THE EAST AND WEST DO MEET

Now turning to the Hindu Bible (the Bhagavad Gita), they say the East and West will never meet. But here is solid evidence that points to the contrary: "And when the yogi engages himself with sincere endeavor in making further progress, being washed of all contaminations (that is the deathless soul, as it was in the beginning) then ultimately achieving perfection after many, many births of practice, he attains the supreme goal."[226] If the soul is individualized Spirit, and in the unrealized man, it is contaminated and when it becomes uncontaminated, now becomes divinity again. It can only mean: the supreme goal points without a doubt to it being reunited with Eternal Spirit. Is it not?

This second quote corroborates the first, but from a much different perspective: "When one's intelligence, mind, faith, and refuge are all fixed in the Supreme, then one becomes fully cleansed of misgivings through complete knowledge and thus proceeds straight on the path of liberation."[227] Here again there is no doubt liberation refers to the immutable, eternal soul. So liberation does not pertain to going to a place (heaven or hell), but rather refers to that level of consciousness where the ultimate union of the individualized soul with Universal Spirit takes place!

THE WORKS THAT I DO

Jesus proclaimed "The works that I do shall he (you) do also!"[228] This exceedingly profound statement can only have a clear, distinct, and logical meaning if we, as so-called mortals, have the same potential to do the same things like he (the son of God) did; prophesying, being clairvoyant, having the power of clairaudience, healing the sick, raising the dead, etc. And as such, it surely seems like we also have the potential to become

---

226 VI:45. (Also cited on page 65).
227 V:17.
228 John 14:12.

even infinitely greater – a "God-man," like him ("the Christ!"). Man to God; no doubt!

ONLY ONE "ABSOLUTE" CAN EXIST

It is a recognizable fact that Jesus is regarded by many as being Divine. In these words of his: "Father... I knew that thou hearest me always: but because of the people which stand by I said it, that they may believe that thou hast sent me."[229]

From this, there is no doubt that there are two distinct and separate parties involved in the conversation. A son, speaking to his Divine Father. But it is utterly impossible for two absolute entities to exist (as already mentioned in chapter fourteen). So if Christ is also regarded as God, this can mean only one thing. The individual divine spark in the Son of man (Jesus often referred to the physical body, including his own, as the Son of man), had expanded to become the Universal Flame of Infinite Divinity – the Christ.[230]

A FITTING CONCLUSION

In closing, there could not be a more fitting way to conclude this volume, than by these timeless words, from Sri Sathya Sai Baba:

"Life is a pilgrimage towards God,
Where man drags his feet
Along the rough and thorny road
Of his years ...
There is no stopping place
In this pilgrimage;

---

229   John 11:41,42.

230   After all, he did say, "He was before Abraham" (John 8:58). This sure seems to be a reference to a former incarnation. As to say this would truly be absurd if he was always divine. For it's self-evident, God existed before all manifestations, as well as, it is totally understood, the Lord created Adam and Eve, before Abraham!

It is one continuous journey,
Through day and night;
Through valley and desert;
Through tears and smiles;
Through death and birth
Through tomb and womb.
When the goal is gained,
Man finds that he has travelled
Only from himself to himself,
That though the way was long and lonesome,
The God that drew him,
Was all the while,
With him and beside him!!!"[231]

---

231 *Sathya Sai Speaks*: Volume VII, page 3. Tustin, California: Sathya Sai Book Center of America, 1993.

Bibliography

THE HOLY BIBLE (CONCORDANCE). KING JAMES VERSION. Cleveland, Ohio: The World Publishing Company.

SATHYA SAI SPEAKS: VOLUME VII. Tustin, California: Sathya Sai Book Center of America, 1993.

http://www.vintagenews.com/2017/12/06/buddy-holly-plane-crash

http://www.adyar.org

http://www.wikipedia.org/wiki/The Day the Music Died

http://www.wikipedia.org/wiki/Theosophical Society

Alder, Vera Stanley. *THE FINDING OF THE THIRD EYE*. Conway Street, London: Rider and Company, 1985. (First published in 1938).

Barclay, William. THE DAILY STUDY BIBLE: THE GOSPEL OF MATTHEW; Volume 2, Chapters 11-28 (Revised Edition). Ontario, Canada: G.R. Welch Co. Ltd., 1975. (First published in Edinburgh, Scotland in 1956 by: The Saint Andrew Press).

Bek, Lilla with Pullar, Philippa. *TO THE LIGHT*. London, England: Unwin Paperbacks, 1985.

Bloomfield, Harold H. and Cain, Michael Peter and Jaffe, Dennis T. and Kory, Robert B. *TM DISCOVERING INNER ENERGY AND OVER-COMING STRESS*. New York, N.Y.: Dell Publishing Co., Inc., 1975.

Carus, Paul and Nyanatiloka, Bhikkhu editors of *BUDDHA: HIS LIFE AND TEACHINGS* (A combination of two books edited by them: *THE GOSPEL OF BUDDHA* and *THE WORD OF THE BUDDHA*). New York, N.Y.: Crescent Books, (published before 1923).

Chinmoy, Sri. *ASTROLOGY, THE SUPERNATURAL AND THE BE-YOND*. Jamaica, New York: Agni Press, 1973.

Chinmoy, Sri. *DEATH AND REINCARNATION: ETERNITY'S VOY-AGE*. Jamaica, New York: Aum Publications, 1997.

Chinmoy, Sri. *MEDITATION: MAN-PERFECTION IN GOD-SAT-ISFACTION*. Jamaica, New York: Agni Press, (fifth printing) 1984.

Choquette, Sonia. *THE PSYCHIC PATHWAY*. New York, N.Y.: Three Rivers Press, 1994.

Dalet, Roger. *RELIEF FROM PAIN WITH FINGER MASSAGE* (translated by L. Zuch). London, England: Hutchinson, 1979.

Das, Lama Surya. *AWAKENING TO THE SACRED*. New York, N.Y.: Broadway Books, 1999.

Ghosh, Sananda Lal. *MEJDA: THE FAMILY AND THE EARLY LIFE OF PARAMAHANSA YOGANANDA*. Los Angeles, California: Self-Realization Fellowship, 1980.

Goswami, Satsvarupa Dasa. *PRABHUPADA*. Vaduz, Lichtenstein; West Germany: The Bhaktivedanta Book Trust, 1983.

Gris, Henry and Dick, William. *THE NEW SOVIET PSYCHIC DIS-COVERIES*. London, England: Sphere Books, 1979.

Guru, Jagad. (Siddhaswarupananda Paramahamsa). *MANTRA MEDI-TATION AND SELF-REALIZATION*. Honolulu, Hawaii: Science of Identity Foundation, 1982.

Haraldsson, Erlendur. *MIRACLES ARE MY VISITING CARDS: AN INVESTIGATIVE REPORT ON THE PSYCHIC PHENOMENA AS-*

SOCIATED WITH SATHYA SAI BABA. London, England: Century Hutchinson Ltd., 1987.

Hatengdi, M.U. *NITYANANDA: THE DIVINE PRESENCE.* Cambridge, Massachusetts: Rudra Press, 1984.

International Society for Krishna Consciousness. *CHANT AND BE HAPPY: THE POWER OF MANTRA MEDITATION.* Los Angeles, California: The Bhaktivedanta Book Trust, 1983.

Krystal, Phyllis. *SAI BABA THE ULTIMATE EXPERIENCE.* Andhra Pradesh, India: Sri Sathya Sai Books and Publications Trust, 1985.

Murphet, Howard. *SAI BABA MAN OF MIRACLES.* York Beach, Maine: Samuel Weiser Inc., 1981.

Osborne, Arthur editor of *THE TEACHINGS OF RAMANA MAHARSHI.* York Beach, Maine: Samuel Weiser, Inc., 1996.

Patchen, Nancy. *THE JOURNEY OF A MASTER SWAMI CHINMAYANANDA: THE MAN, THE PATH, THE TEACHING.* Berkeley, California: Asian Humanities Press, 1989.

Paulson, Genevieve Lewis. *KUNDALINI AND THE CHAKRAS: A PRACTICAL MANUAL: EVOLUTION IN THIS LIFETIME.* St. Paul, Minnesota: Llewellyn Publications, (fifth printing) 1994.

Prabhupada, A.C. Bhaktivedanta Swami. *BHAGAVAD GITA AS IT IS.* Sydney, Australia: The Bhaktivedanta Book Trust, 1986. (First published in 1983).

Prasad, R.C. editor and translator of Tulasidasa's *SRI RAMACARITAMANASA: THE HOLY LAKE OF THE ACTS OF RAMA.* Delhi. India: Motilal Banarsidass Publishers, 1999.

Rampa, T. Lobsang. *THE THIRD EYE.* New York, N.Y.: Ballantine Books, 1993 (twenty-sixth printing). {First published by Brandt and Brandt in 1956}.

Rampa, T. Lobsang. *YOU FOREVER.* York Beach, Maine: Samuel Weiser Inc., 1990.

Ryan, Sara Regina. *ONLY GOD: A BIOGRAPHY OF YOGI RAMSU-RATKUMAR.* Prescott, Arizona: Hohm Press, 2004.

Sandweiss, Samuel H. *SAI BABA THE HOLY MAN AND THE PSYCHI-ATRIST.* San Diego, California: Birth Day Publishing Company, 1975.

Starck, Marcia. *HEALING WITH ASTROLOGY.* New Delhi, India: Health and Harmony, a division of B. Jain Publishers. (First Indian Edition) 1998.

White, Ruth with Gildas. *A MESSAGE OF LOVE: A CHANNELLED GUIDE TO OUR FUTURE.* Windmill Street, London: Judy Piatkus Publishers Ltd., 1994.

Yogananda, Paramahansa. *AUTOBIOGRAPHY OF A YOGI.* Los Angeles, California: Self-Realization Fellowship, 2010. Thirteenth edition 1998. (First published in 1946).

Yogananda, Paramahansa. *MAN'S ETERNAL QUEST.* Los Angeles, California: Self-Realization Fellowship, 1982.

Yogananda, Paramahansa. *THE DIVINE ROMANCE.* Los Angeles, California: Self-Realization Fellowship, 2005. (First edition—2000).

Yogananda, Paramahansa. THE YOGA OF JESUS. Los Angeles, California: Self-Realization Fellowship, 2009.

Yukteswar, Swami Sri. *THE HOLY SCIENCE.* Los Angeles, California: Self-Realization Fellowship, 1984. (Written in 1894).

Lightning Source UK Ltd.
Milton Keynes UK
UKHW010639100820
367987UK00002B/311